# PRAISE

"Lisa's love of travel and her fierce determination to push all boundaries, takes the reader with her on a thoughtful, fun and fearless journey. Lisa opens herself and the reader to the world and explores with courage, the physical world around her and the philosophical world within."

— Maureen Wheeler, founder Lonely Planet

"These stories transport the reader to exotic places all over the world yet encapsulate iconic moments in an American life that any woman will recognize. From quirky teenager to adventurous mother, Alpine's audacity shocks us in a way that makes us wish we had been following in her footsteps all these years. Lisa Alpine is an unabashed combination of Graham Greene and Isadora Duncan with runaway stories that are charming and disheveled snapshots of an unapologetically wild life."

— Carla King, Misadventures Media

# WILD LIFE

# WILD LIFE

## TRAVEL ADVENTURES OF A WORLDLY WOMAN

Lisa Alpine

a collection of too-true stories

DANCING WORDS PRESS

*Wild Life: Travel Adventures of a Worldly Woman*
Copyright © Lisa Alpine, 2014
First published in the United States of America by
Dancing Words Press

Requests for permission should be made via email to:
Dancing Words Press
www.LisaAlpine.com

I have tried to recreate events, locales and conversations from my
memories of them. In order to maintain their anonymity in some
instances I have changed the names of individuals and places, I may
have changed some identifying characteristics and details such as
physical properties, occupations and places of residence.

ISBN 978-0-9842293-6-9

Cover image: "The Almost Circus and Invisible Audience" by
photographer Brooke Shaden  www.brookeshaden.com

Book and cover design: Scott Jordan and Lisa Alpine

Printed in the United States of America
Copyright © 2014 Lisa Alpine, All rights reserved.

# DEDICATION

This book is dedicated to the women who encouraged me to reach for my dreams, which resulted in a lifelong pursuit of adventure travel. To name a few:

Grandma Lucy, who gave birth to my uncle in a mining camp and rode a black stallion with reckless abandon across the Atacama Desert in Chile.

Ilene Chapin, who surrounded herself with music, art, and gay men.

Jo Dean, a housewife from Sunnyvale who shot and killed a man while working undercover for the Red Cross in France during WWII.

My high school history teacher, who took me to a state historical convention in Oroville. At night we went to a roadhouse and danced to a country-western band. She pulled an electric yoyo from her purse, selling them for $10 apiece as she spun them in glowing neon arcs around the dance floor. Amazingly, she didn't knock anybody out.

Maxine Baker for passing on her ecstatic dancing blood and giving me up for adoption because she was way too wild to raise a child.

And most of all, to my adopted mom, Phyllis Richards McCreery, who loved me unconditionally and never complained when I departed solo on trips with no known return date to places not even on maps. I would look back when I was boarding the plane and there Mom stood, tears running down her face, trying to wave and smile and look bright but she was so sad. She never knew when she would see me again, yet she always let me go and waited for me to return.

# CONTENTS

# INTRODUCTION

A teenage girl lies supine under the Southern Cross, waves gently swooshing at the edges of her bare feet. The white sand beach cool under her body. The tropical sun departed hours before. She stares upward, pinned to the earth under the weight of darkness punctured by a plump, opalescent moon.

The moon is just a hole in the tent, beckoning her to peek through and awaken to the infinite light that shines on every detail of creation—joy and sorrow, pain and suffering. Words woven in foreign tongues. Desert sand dunes and mangrove swamps. Diesel-fumed cities and moss-draped forests.

Can she wrap her mind around this vastness and not be afraid of the incomprehensible yet tangible reality of the cosmos' boundlessness?

An inner assuring voice whispers, "Don't be afraid of what you can't see. Come, explore."

*The moon is just a hole in the tent*
*And the stars are where the cloth wore thin*

The night this simple verse came to me, I was 15, on vacation with my family on the Big Island of Hawai'i.

It was a jasmine-scented evening. Big-boned, bronze-skinned women in hibiscus-print muumuus slowly danced the hula as my parents sipped mai tais. The rustle clack of palm fronds and the potent scent of night-blooming jasmine lured me down to the crescent-shaped beach beyond the circle of family and the halo of restaurant lights. I slipped away from the lilting strum and thrum of ukuleles, down the lava-stone steps, onto the beach and into the darkness. Trade winds caressed my skin and lulled my restless teenage spirit. I lay down on the smooth sand, mesmerized by the largest night sky I had ever seen.

The grandeur of the Milky Way's swathe was unadulterated by the glare of city lights. Through the full moon overhead, the cosmos shared its secret and a poem was born. The reality of infinity dawned like a clap of thunder—the universe reached in all directions with no end and no beginning. It was biblical, without all the commandments and old, bearded men.

This stark and magical moment in my evolution erupted in me a desire to roam open-ended through unfamiliar cultures and geographies.

Armchair travelers ask why I left home at the age of 18—the day I graduated from high school—to vagabond around Europe and the Middle East, South America, Africa, Indonesia, the South Pacific. Places in the world sometimes unbearable yet always intriguing. I respond that I'm a nomad, despite my upbringing in a middle-class, suburban American family, and I'm happiest when rambling through foreign cultures. Who needs a spaceship to discover new galaxies when the world offers such a full and infinite embrace?

The tales contained in *Wild Life* are woven from the threads of wanderlust that are the fabric of my life. I am a woman who wanders and wonders and writes. I have no room for souvenirs in my backpack, but I do have stories to share and a desire to tell them.

These stories meander from the savanna of the Masai Mara to the ski resorts of Switzerland. Initiations, dreams, and visions shadow and illuminate the exotic landscapes in which these journeys take place.

Enjoy the trip!
Lisa
Mill Valley California, 2014

# LICKING MONET

Paris 1972

Alone on the naugahyde bench. No one else in the gallery. Midwinter in Paris. I'm a student studying Monet's "Water Lilies." The wall-size paintings circle me like a wagon standoff in a Western movie. My gaze softens, drawn into the azure waters that embrace the languid lilies. So many hues of blue. Pale robin's egg, mosaic pieces of shimmering sea glass, bruised forget-me-not petals.

I stand and walk slowly up to the beckoning canvas, looking around the still-empty oval room in the Musée de l'Orangerie. Inside, I am alone in the warm womb of springtime, imagining lotus blossoms delicately perfuming the gallery. Outside, multitudes of frosty crystals blanket the barren gardens of the Tuileries.

Inching forward until my nose almost touches the painting. Does this pond have a scent? Yes, a bouquet of sunlight and sugar tinged with an algae-like mustiness. So close now, my breath meets the canvas. Dust motes gathered on tiny, dried brushstrokes of mineraly oil paint blend with whiffs of piney turpentine.

It is not enough to gaze and sniff. Does beauty have a taste? This pageant of floral sirens blooming in the midst of monochromatic winter is intoxicating. I'm seduced by a kaleidoscope of mossy jades, liquid sapphires, and blushing garnets; enticed into an enchanted realm of dancing and bejeweled water sprites.

Impulsively, my lips part.

My tongue tip snakes toward the water lilies and licks. The paint's hard ridges are rough—there is no flavor. I retreat, but I'm overwhelmed with the desire to taste art. To be art. To not be separated from beauty, but to dive headfirst into the blues, lavenders, and pinks of the painter's symphony.

Lingering in the pond of Monet's ode to eternal spring, the cool waters swirl inside me, the lily pads bump against my interior; I move like blue water; I feel the pastel petals shimmer on my skin. The translucent blossoms rise from the pond on their emerald stems and unfurl in my heart.

I like this new way of being art. Tomorrow: the Rodin Museum... .

# AUTHOR'S NOTE

This story was inspired by Cheryl Strayed, author of *Wild: Lost and Found on the Pacific Crest Trail,* at a writing workshop. She prompted us to write for ten minutes about a time when we went too far, or about an object or action that we were reluctant to include in our stories. Hence—my confession.

# RADA'S BLOOM

Austria 1972

*We who lived in concentration camps can remember the men who walked through the huts comforting others, giving away their last piece of bread. They may have been few in number, but they offer sufficient proof that everything can be taken from a man but one thing: the last of human freedoms — to choose one's attitude in any given set of circumstances — to choose one's own way.[1]* — Viktor E. Frankl

Cold drizzle in summer. I arrived in the heart of Vienna hoping to find a bed at the youth hostel. Full. Then, I wandered over to the *Stadtpark* (public park). Grizzled bums occupied the benches, lolling in a cloud of fruity schnapps fumes. I didn't feel comfortable sleeping there, so I strolled along Europe's longest shopping boulevard,

*Mariahilfer Strasse,* to the *Wien Westbahnhof* (the main train station). As I walked along the same wide promenade that Hitler triumphantly marched down in 1938, I asked strangers if they could recommend a cheap place to spend the night.

It was the summer of 1972. I was 18 years old, blond, wearing nondescript jeans, a raggedy t-shirt, and ported a small backpack. Hitchhiking from Denmark, I was lured south by the sun-ripe peaches and beaches of Greece. Passing through Germany, Austria, and soon, Yugoslavia, then skirting Albania into Greece with its tantalizingly chalk-white cliff islands and aquamarine sea. Motivated to the edge of the Mediterranean by Joni Mitchell's "Carey," a song from her 1971 album *Blue.* It was inspired by her time with a cave-dwelling hippie community in the village of Matala, on the Greek island of Crete. It was my siren's call to the caves of Crete, the stark white-blue of Santorini, to bonfire nights fueled by retsina and ouzo, to dancing under a cat-eye moon. Far away from drizzly weather, grey skies, and Teutonic attitudes.

Not one of the business-suit-clad people clicking by in their shiny patent leather shoes offered any helpful suggestions. I began to feel invisible. I was considering hitchhiking out of the city, even though it was dusk, and finding a place to camp out on the side of the *Autobahn* in a grassy ditch (it would not be the first time), when a short woman in a grey cardigan walked up to me and asked, "Do you need help?" She was as tall as my shoulder. I looked down into her wrinkly, smiling face and realized she was speaking English. Good English that I could understand, which was uncommon.

"I'm looking for an inexpensive place to spend the night."

She continued to peer up at me and said, "Let's go get coffee at the train station café."

Getting out of the rain seemed like a good idea, even though she had not mentioned anything about where I might sleep.

We walked two blocks to the café and chatted over rich, cream-topped Viennese coffee, a glass of water, and a newspaper. She told me she had lived in Chicago and that is where she learned English.

Her name was Rada Milovich.

When our coffee cups were drained, she said, "Would you like to come home with me?" She was staring at me through cloudy bifocals.

"Okay. I only need a place to sleep for one night, as I'm hitching to Yugoslavia tomorrow. Where do you live?"

"In another district, but we can walk there."

And walk and walk we did. The wide boulevards shrunk to pot-holed streets, the sidewalks cracked and carpeted with gangly weeds. Storefronts disappeared and warehouses took their place as I followed her sturdy march. Broken streetlights failed to provide light in the waning dusk. The evening strollers and café-goers had disappeared and we were the only pedestrians, our footsteps echoing through the shabby, deserted street.

She suddenly turned and went down an alley, motioning me to follow her, and then opened the metal door to a building with no windows. I would never have followed her here if she was not a tiny, grey-haired old lady with an impish grin.

Up three flights of clanking metal stairs, and then through a door that opened into a grey-washed hallway with a yellow light bulb hanging from the ceiling, providing an eerie glow. It recurred to me that maybe I should have hitchhiked out of town.

Rada opened the door to her apartment with a thin, bent key. She did not offer any excuses as to the dingy living quarters. Or to the motley-brown rat that scurried down the hallway before we entered.

"Come in. You are my first visitor."

Somehow that did not surprise me.

It was a one-room studio with a bathroom. There were no adornments on the walls or trinkets on the bureau. Plain. Clean but rundown. I hesitantly set my backpack down as she made us tea. We chatted for a while but she was tired and wanted to go to bed. I helped her unfold the convertible sofa bed we had been sitting on, and began to lay out my sleeping bag on the bare floor.

Rada appeared in a simple white nightgown and climbed into bed. She looked up at me and said sternly, "No, no. You must sleep in the bed with me, not on the floor!"

It was odd and uncomfortable sharing a bed with a person I had just met a few hours before. But it was only for one night and she was harmless. A faint whistle-snore escaped her. In the dim light of the room, she looked so peaceful as she fell into slumber. The sheets were neatly folded over the threadbare blanket edge and her arms were resting on top of the sheet. Her face calm, haloed in wispy grey hair. I decided it was good to be here and looked back over at Rada before I, too, prepared to succumb to sleep. Then, startled, my eyes focused. I saw the numbers in faded bluish ink tattooed on the inside of her left forearm. The numbers her cardigan sleeve had concealed.

I'd never met a Holocaust survivor.

Deeply disturbed, I didn't fall asleep until she scurried out of bed in the bleak light of dawn. She pulled her cardigan back on immediately and left. Awhile later, she burst through the door, seemingly propelled by a wave of damp, frigid air trailed by the yeasty aroma of fresh baked bread that filled her tiny apartment. She had gone to the bakery to get our breakfast.

This would be the first of many mornings of racing to the bakery to see who could buy breakfast. This sprint was ridiculous. Rada rose at 6 AM, and then, after I beat her to it one day, at 5 AM she'd pop up, raring to be the first to the bakery. I didn't want her spending her meager pension feeding me, but I also didn't want to walk in the pitch dark down those haunted streets. I kept promising her I would stay yet another day if she would let me purchase the warm, crusty rolls and butter we noshed on around her pill-box-size Formica table.

The days stretched on as she showed me Vienna. We walked the city and sat on park benches, feeding the pigeons. We talked over coffee and then we talked some more when we would lie beside each other in the dark on the sagging sofa bed.

Her stories were what kept me there. As we got to know each other, she told me about the origin of the etched numbers on the thin skin of her arm. About her time in Auschwitz and the family she had lost.

9

She told the stories in vivid, gripping detail but without bitterness or anger. She brought to life the sounds of the harsh, screeching grate of the rusty cattle car doors as they slid open; the scuffling noises of boots and worn shoe leather meeting the ground as her family was shoved out of the trains and into the camp. The unfolding of the chapters from this horrific period in her life took days. Intertwined with the nightmare were also happy memories of her earlier life in Czechoslovakia, her homeland.

Had she ever told anyone else about the tragedy of slowly losing her entire family? Her daughter, her son, her husband, her sisters, her mother and father. And then surviving Auschwitz all by herself? Was I the first?

"Why didn't you go back to your country after the war?" I asked.

"I can't go back. My village was destroyed and I have no family or friends left there. The borders are closed to my kind. Czechoslovakia is lost to me."

One day I asked, "Rada, the day I met you, you told me you learned English in Chicago. How did you end up there?"

She became reflective and then said, "I was evacuated from the camp and the Red Cross arranged for me to go to America and live with a sponsor. I took a job as a nanny and learned English, but I never fit in. I knew no one. I'm a Jew from Eastern Europe. Always. Austria is closer to my country, so I moved back here."

In the two weeks I stayed with her I never saw or heard another resident in the hallway. I wondered if she was squatting. She told me it was government housing that was offered to her as a Holocaust survivor.

We went to the train station and drank coffee daily. She liked watching the people. She was keen on staring at the immigrants with their shabby, bulging suitcases as they got off the trains coming from Eastern Bloc countries. She could tell which country they were from by their appearance.

"That fellow wearing a cap is from Hungary. That one in the blue work shirt is from Romania."

It surprised me that she liked hanging out at the train station café, considering it was a train that took her through the gates of hell to the concentration camp. I asked her why she kept coming here and she said, "I hope to see someone I know from my village."

One day, a lovely lattice-topped Linzer Torte was placed before Rada and me between our coffee cups and saucers. The waitress indicated that a customer had paid for it and sent it over as a surprise. We looked around the café for him, but he had left. After a steady diet of crusty, warm rolls and butter, this was Technicolor flavor. Symphonic, sweet-yet-tart red currant jam crowned the lush cake layer of aromatic ground hazelnuts and butter.

Rada leaned forward to hear my groans of pleasure and beamed as I fingered the streaks of red currant jam off the plate and licked my fingertips.

She said, "The Linzer Torte recipe is the oldest-known in the world and is one of the most famous Viennese culinary specialties."

She continued, "I worked briefly in a bakery and learned how to make it. It is a very crumbly pastry made of flour, unsalted butter, egg yolks, lemon zest, cinnamon, and ground hazelnuts, covered with a filling of red currant

11

jam. It is covered by a lattice of pastry crust on top of the preserves."

Rada chuckled and said, "I was not a very good baker, as I would improvise and not follow the recipes, but I did enjoy eating the tortes we baked. It was too tempting and I was still so scrawny from my internment in Auschwitz. It was the only time I was fat in my entire life. I think that is what got me fired."

Rada's sunny temperament turned morose and subdued when she sensed I was getting ready to depart. Those white sand beaches and late-night *mazurkas* were calling me south. The greys of Rada's apartment and the city streets were starting to weigh on me. I needed peaches, grapes, blue seas, and other young people. She could feel my restlessness as I sat beside her on the park bench. It made her sad, and she even had a temper tantrum, accusing me of abandoning her.

But leave I did. She was anxious about my hitchhiking, so I had compromised and bought a train ticket to Zagreb. After one last coffee, she walked with me to the departure platform and waved goodbye. For years I wrote her letters and sent postcards from exotic locales, but then she stopped responding.

Twenty-three years after meeting Rada, I visited Auschwitz. Four other journalists and I, all of us well-known in the American river rafting community, had been invited to Poland to attend the 54th Annual International Kayak Rally on the Dunajec River that borders Slovakia. On our one free day, the Krakow Tourist Board planned to take us on a tour of the salt mines. I had another plan. I wanted to visit Auschwitz. Rada's stories were imprinted on my heart.

It was a mutiny, as the entire kayak team wanted to go with me instead of to the salt mines. The tourist board representatives rebuked my desire, but ended up arranging for a bus to take us there. They weren't keen on American journalists viewing this particular epoch of Poland's history.

The countryside was verdant with leafing trees and spring-green grass. As we approached the gates of Auschwitz, the terrain turned brown and sterile. Not a bush or blade of grass. Just barren soil. A tour guide led us through the dank warehouses, many storing the items guards confiscated from the newly arrived prisoners. One warehouse was just shoes and shoes. Another housed thousands of suitcases stacked to the ceiling, taken from people being pushed out of the cattle cars onto the hard-packed soil and into the camp surrounded by barbed wire. Our tour guide pointed out her own suitcase. A beam of dull light shone on this battered leather bag. Dust motes dancing on the light beam were the only movement in the cavernous building as we stood there, paralyzed with grief and shock. She survived Auschwitz just as Rada had—alone. I wondered if one of the suitcases belonged to Rada or her family.

We walked in silence, heads down and hearts aching, to our bus. Through my tears I saw wheat fields top-heavy with seed heads stretching for miles beside the road. Punctuating the green sea were bright, lipstick-red wild poppies. Their delicate petals fluttered in the breeze like miniature prayer flags on their tall stems. I saw these as evidence that the river of sorrow that had streamed from the camps decades ago had saturated the countryside, the crimson blood metamorphosed into flowers of beauty and cheer.

I asked the bus driver to stop and I went out into the chest-high wheat field and picked the poppy heads. Up close, the flowers were the same color as the red currant jam spread over the Linzer Torte that Rada and I had shared over two decades before.

Folded into a sock in my luggage, the seeds came home with me to California. I planted them in pots beside my pool. Soon, the summer heat coaxed the seedlings to sprout and grow. Each pot was filled with statuesque scarlet poppies. It was odd, though, because the next year, they morphed and the blooms were cornflower-blue on shorter stalks. The year after that, they were white and shaped like stars.

The seeds have spread and naturalized, and they now carpet my garden, blooming pure white.

I researched the true name of this special poppy that has kept Rada's memory alive in my garden. Its name is *Papaver rhoeas*, the red-flowered corn poppy. It is a native of Europe, and is notable as an agricultural weed and as a symbol of fallen soldiers. It is the flower of wartime remembrance.

1: Viktor E. Frankl, *Man's Search For Meaning*. Beacon's Press, 1959.

# FRENCH THE HARD WAY

Switzerland 1973

*"Vide la poubelle et ferme les volets!"*

A squat, ugly woman hovers over me, poking me in the arm to wake me up. Again, she shrills in harsh Swiss-German-accented French, "Empty the waste basket and close the shutters!"

Rising from the somnambulant depths of a bone-tired sleep, the clock beside the bed glows neon-green, indicating it is four in the morning.

Who is this nasty person with spittle spraying from her mouth as she scowls at me? Perhaps a really bad dream with a sharp pointer finger?

No, unfortunately, she is my new roommate and threatens, "You had better get up and do what I say," followed by more emphatic pokes.

Hoping she will disappear, I empty the wastebasket and close the blinds and crawl back in bed to catch a few more hours' sleep before I have to go to work. I still don't know her name.

*Mon dieu*! As if my life isn't difficult enough at this moment. Trapped in a job that is one step above slavery, anemic from a diet of liver and peas (dietary hell for a vegetarian), and depressed over being treated like a second-class citizen. Now this—a troll-bitch roommate.

Life had been peachy just a short while ago.

Dreams of moving to Paris and living *la vie bohème* had come to fruition ten months earlier when I flew to the City of Light two weeks after my eighteenth birthday. I had never been out of the United States but my parents, who thought this was a fanciful *Moveable-Feast*-inspired pipe dream, gave me their blessing wisely woven with a few contingencies. I bankrolled my exodus from Sunnyvale, California and arranged all the travel plans plus came up with a study program that would give me some semblance of student life.

Accomplishing all of the above, I lived in Paris, studying art history at the Sorbonne. One morning, as I sat through another boring lecture given by a wizened professor (which I barely understood due to my rudimentary French), I looked out the windows onto the sidewalk. It was spring and chestnut tree blossoms delicately floated through the gentle, warm breeze. Like a restless caged animal, I rose from the hard wood seat and abandoned my moldy textbooks. Wanderlust had awakened and sent me hitchhiking all over Europe for the next six months until I ran out of money in Greece.

Rumor had it on the European backpacker trail that there were seasonal jobs at the Swiss ski resorts. As the

Aegean waters chilled and my cash diminished with the shortening days, I optimistically journeyed north, even though I'd never seen snow or knew how to ski.

The first rent in the fabric of my happiness was the telegram I received from my parents at the American Express office in Vienna. "Your best friend Jan Russell died in a head-on car collision this week. Her parents want to know if you ever discussed her religious beliefs or burial preferences. They do not know if she would like to be cremated or buried."

Sobs racked me as I collapsed on the marble tile floor.

No, we had not discussed these existential quandaries. We talked boys and Paris. I lay there on the concrete, the telegram crumpled beside me. She had been saving her money waitressing at a diner so she could join me in Europe.

My heart was heavy with grief. I would never see her again. In shock, dazed and confused I continued hitchhiking to Switzerland.

Things lightened up a few days later when a plush Rolls-Royce stopped to give me a ride on the road skirting Lake Geneva. This was a first. Most times it was students in dented Citroën *deux chevauxs* or workers in mini delivery trucks who gave me lifts.

"I'm going to Villars-sur-Ollon. Throw your pack in the back seat and hop on in," said the youthful driver, who sported a black chauffeur cap, Hawaiian shirt, and jeans.

"Where are you from?" he asked in an American accent.

He was my kind of good-looking with black hair, blue eyes, and a big smile.

I sat in the front seat with him and chatted about job options for vagabonds like myself.

He said, "You should come to Villars with me. It's a hoity-toity ski resort in the Vaudoises Alps above Montreux and overlooks the Rhône Valley with views of Mont Blanc. They probably need ski instructors."

"I actually can't ski. Maybe I can find another type of job?"

He looked at me and laughed because I was going to a ski resort but couldn't ski. "Well, my boss is looking for a nanny. Interested?"

My only experience baby-sitting kids as a teenager had been a nightmare, so this didn't seem appealing until he said who he worked for.

Nodding in a non-committal way, he continued, "Yeah, I drive for Keith Richards of the Rolling Stones and his family. It's pretty easy as they don't go out much. I was working at a gas station in Villars after bumming around Europe for a year and they offered me a job while I pumped gas for them."

The nanny job suddenly had appeal. I said, "Sure, sounds good."

As we wound up the twisty mountain road, he said, "Keith and Mick come here every year and get full blood transfusions from a famous doctor."

I had no idea what he was talking about but it didn't matter.

We drove straight to a classic-looking Swiss chalet at the end of a valley surrounded by dairy farms. Red geraniums in flower boxes lined each windowsill and snow blanketed the roof. He parked in the circular driveway and went inside to ask them about me and the nanny job while I waited in the Rolls.

In less than five minutes he waved me into a grand wood-paneled foyer that opened up into a cavernous living room accented with Persian carpets and splashy floral arrangements. Hand-hewn beams rose above the stone fireplace you could stand in and piles of toys littered the room. It was a little overwhelming after living out of my backpack and staying in cramped hostel rooms for seven months.

Keith's Italian girlfriend and mother of his two children, Anita Pallenberg, waltzed in barefoot in a sexy lace vintage dress and shook my hand. She was sleek and beautiful, though she had dark circles under her eyes and her fingernails were chewed to the quick. We sat on overstuffed leather sofas and the job interview began with questions about where I was from and did I like kids. She didn't seem bothered by the fact that I was barely past kidhood myself.

Then she got more specific about the job requirements. In a flawless proper British accent she said, "The entire family usually stays up all night while Keith and his musician friends party and write music. You will need to keep the same hours."

I nodded my head in agreement.

She continued, "We also travel to an island in the Caribbean where Keith records and you will be expected to come with us."

*Yes, yes, and yes!* I kept nodding my head.

Anita didn't seem interested in conversing with me— just giving me the job rundown. She stood up, yawned, and looked directly at me for the first time and said, "Well, do you want the job?"

Startled, I said, "I do. When do I start?"

As she walked out of the room, she turned slightly and said over her shoulder, "Tomorrow is fine. The kids' names are Marlon and Dandelion."

"Looks like you got the job," said my handsome chauffeur savior who was waiting for me in the driveway as I hopped into the seat beside him and planted a big kiss on his cheek. "My wife will be thrilled. She was offered that job so we could work together but it didn't pan out because of the hours, the kids were a bit difficult, and she's pregnant."

*Oh, a wife.* Well, at least I had a job.

He dropped me off in town, where I decided to check into the youth hostel for my one night before working for the stars. I went to the ski bar for a glass of celebratory champagne, spending my last two dollars. On a stool nearby was the rubbery-lipped profile of Mick Jagger sipping a Scotch whiskey. Feeling upbeat, I nodded in his direction. He ignored me, but I knew that soon Mick and I would be on a first-name basis.

My euphoria continued as I strolled in the dusky afternoon sun down the main shopping street in Villars, admiring all the fancy store windows displaying luxuries like diamond necklaces, French perfumes, cashmere sweaters, and boxes of chocolate all far beyond my budget but lovely to look at through the plate glass. I pulled my Greek wool fisherman's sweater tighter around me as snowflakes lightly dusted the sidewalk.

Looking up, I saw the highly polished black Rolls-

Royce coming toward me. It stopped in the middle of the road. Just as I was about to go over and say hello to my chauffeur buddy, wondering at the coincidence of seeing him again today, the passenger door flew open and a hail storm of glossy designer shopping bags were pitched onto the cobblestones, bouncing and skittering across the street. Then a high-pitched scream emanated from inside the limo. With tanned long legs, and her dress pulled up to her thighs, Anita sprung out of the car, howling at my driver friend in completely incomprehensible Italian, her perfect English evaporated.

She didn't notice that everyone—drivers, pedestrians and shopkeepers—were gaping at her hysterical display. My bewildered friend begged her to get back in the car, though it made no difference as she continued to shriek at no one in particular. She picked up her pile of bags and flounced down the street toward me. The chauffeur, looking as confused as everyone else, got back in the car and drove away, shaking his head.

As Anita approached, I backed away before she could recognize me. I realized there was no way I was going to work for such an out-of-control maniac bitch.

Well, back to the drawing board with less than a franc in my pocket.

Returning to the bar/restaurant where I had just been celebrating my new job, I smiled wanly at the bartender and inquired in halting French if they were hiring.

He nodded and pointed to a door behind the bar and said to go talk to the boss.

The room was dark and smelled of cigar smoke. A large, bald man in a cheap suit sat at a wooden desk and asked in French what I wanted.

Once again, on the same day, I found myself being interviewed.

Mr. Choca introduced himself in choppy English once he realized I was American but didn't shake my hand or invite me to sit down. He told me there was a waitress job available immediately at his crepe house a few kilometers up the mountain at the ski lodge. He did not ask if I had ever waitressed before and didn't seem to care that my ability to speak French was extremely limited.

He asked for my passport and put it in his desk, turning the key to lock the drawer, and mentioned something about getting a medical exam. He assumed I had accepted the job, though I had not even had time to nod my head affirmatively or say *oui*.

I did manage to find out it paid $150 a month and included room, board, and a ski pass. Mr. Choca then briskly told me meals were served in the basement and I would be escorted to my lodgings after dinner by one of the other waitresses. He waved me off toward the door and went back to his bookkeeping.

I practically skipped out of his office, imagining myself learning French while serving Chantilly crepes to happy, well-heeled, rosy-cheeked jetsetters. Plus learning to ski and eating fondue while drinking schnapps in my off-work hours with handsome, debonair, world-wise men.

Early that evening, definitely hungry, I sussed out where dinner was being served to the staff. Down a flight of stairs behind the bar was a long, dark hall with a trestle table where a dozen employees already sat down in front of their meal.

Might as well start practicing my French. I nudged onto the plank bench in between two older women wearing babushkas and said, "*Bon soir, je suis Américain. Comment allez-vous?*"

Maybe I didn't say the greeting correctly but no one responded or looked at me. Then a surly, bearded man plopped a metal dining plate in front of me with a clank. On its scratched surface was a mound of overcooked military green peas accompanied by a thin, grayish slice of liver.

"Dinner?" I asked my sullen companions, who still ignored me.

This was not good. I was a vegetarian. A young and hungry vegetarian. The van Gogh painting "The Potato Eaters" of peasants eating a meal in a dimly lit room was coming to life before my eyes.

A cute kid seated across from me, no more than fourteen years old, who looked like he might be a Gypsy, winked and stuck his finger in his mouth to imitate gagging. I laughed and tried to start up a conversation with him but he spoke only Spanish. Everyone around me looked tired and rough around the edges, all eating in leaden silence. They, too, seemed to speak only Spanish, or Italian. No Swiss and certainly no Americans.

By the end of the meal, which I didn't touch, I patched together the story behind this collective of downtrodden workers, who came here seasonally year-in-year-out to work menial jobs for Choca. They were migrant workers—not students like me, cobbling together pocket change for their next backpack adventure. They weren't here to ski or learn French. They were work slaves expecting nothing more than minimum wage, slop for food, and fourteen-hour work shifts.

And now I was one of them.

Shown to my drafty bunkroom by one of the non-communicative babushka women from dinner, stomach growls sang me to sleep.

First item on the agenda the next morning was to visit Choca in his office. He was very surprised to see me again. Right off the bat, I decided to set things straight. "Mr. Choca, I am a vegetarian. I do not eat meat. How about if I cook my own food at the dorm and you give me a food allowance since I won't be eating downstairs?"

A calm silence followed as he digested my request. Then he laughed and said, "You want me to pay for your extra food? You're nuts!"

Ha ha ha. He continued to chuckle.

Miffed at his complete lack of regard for my needs, I shuffled out of his office and continued up the mountain to the crepe house for on-site job training. Maybe I could eat some crepes during the slow periods.

A stocky, commanding woman with wiry salt-and-pepper hair that sprung straight up from her head greeted me at the door and threw an apron in my face. She huffed that I was *"trop tard!"* Too late!

If she had had a broom she would have hit me with it. In fast and furious French, she ordered me about with utter disdain. I understood only ten percent of what she was spitting at me. In between trying to figure out what she was telling me to do and attempting to ignore the hunger pangs triggered by the buttery-skillet aroma of crepes, I wondered if she hated blonds, Americans, or everyone that Choca sent her way.

From setting tables to folding napkins, I could not do anything right. At least in her book. By the end of my shift, I was so upset at being yelled at in a language that I didn't understand that I collapsed in the stock room, hidden from sight, and sobbed uncontrollably. The only thing I wanted was my mom to hug and feed me, and for this nightmare to be over.

By the end of the second day on the job, I had become überwaitress. I'd intuit what the customers were ordering and smile and rush and deliver. People seemed happy with my service and the bossy training lady had disappeared. This wasn't so bad. I marveled at the sweeping views from the floor-to-ceiling windows looking out on snow-topped Alpine peaks. I'd sneak bites of Gruyére cheese crepes and strain to learn the French that was spoken to me. The customers were initially cold toward me, but once I laughed or joked—my language skills were accelerating out of sheer need for survival—they warmed up and would ask where I was from.

Every time I handed them the menu, though, a pang of annoyance coursed through me because at the bottom of the laminated menu placard was a lie—a single phrase that stated, "Pourboire inclus." I had deciphered what it meant: Tip included. Well, I never got a tip. The management was pocketing them.

My resentment toward Choca was escalating.

Then, a week later, the roommate from hell appeared in the middle of the night and things spun totally out of control. Not only did Choca have me waitressing at the crepe house but also bartending at the discothèque located in the ski lodge at night—another job I was unqualified to do, as I'd never made a drink in my life. Luckily, the ski crowd seemed to only guzzle Johnnie Walker *Rouge* or *Noir*. Pour the golden liquor in a glass and push it across the bar. At first I was psyched to work in the disco because I loved to dance. It didn't register that I would now be pulling fourteen-hour shifts working both at the crepe house during the day and the disco till the wee hours, with not a whole lot of energy left for dancing.

The other downside was that the club was empty, cold, and boring, and I was by myself doing all the work—bartendress, DJ, and dishwasher. No one came there because the drinks were too expensive and the bar was perched too high up on the mountain on a narrow, windy road above the village of Villars, which twinkled far below.

Nightly, I trudged in a tired trance down the hill back to my dorm in town. Sometimes, though, the half-hour walk was magical with the moon and stars sparkling on the crystalline snow banks. I had never been in the snow before so this captivated me. I'd sleep till noon and then wake too fatigued to use my ski pass. And my charming roommate snored. Loudly, like a guffawing circus clown.

She was from poor Germanic peasant stock and had zero social skills. She looked like she was in her thirties but, I found out later, was my age. Not only did we share accommodations, but she also waitressed at the crepe house. Probably because she spoke passable French.

She was a lousy waitress and customers, scared of her perma-scowl and surly nature, would push their tables over the invisible line of demarcation to my serving area. This did not endear me to her and also doubled my workload.

After several weeks of this, I'd had it! I wasn't learning to ski. I was being abused by the ornery and envious troll bitch—though I was getting a handle on speaking French, but a lot of it was derogatory phrases from being yelled at. This was not how I was used to being treated.

Maybe that baby-sitting job for the famous heroin addicts was still available. Staying up all night long corralling spoiled children and fending off the tight-leather-panted rock-and-rollers suddenly wasn't sounding like such a bad work option.

Again, I marched into Choca's office in the back of the bar/restaurant and announced, "I'm quitting."

He swiveled his head toward me, a snide smile spreading across his face, and said, "You will work until the end of the ski season. I have your passport. You will get it back in March."

"What? I didn't agree to this slavery."

"Too bad."

"So you aren't going to let me leave?"

He picked at his cuticles and without looking up, curtly said, "*Mais, non.*"

In disbelief, I stomped out of his office.

*Okay, bastard. If you won't let me quit, I will make you fire me.*

As I stood on the sidewalk pondering how to liberate myself from Choca's chokehold, a jingly, horse-drawn carriage passed by in the street. It was Rafi, a vagabonder from Israel on the seasonal job trail who I had befriended earlier. He was on the clock, taking tourists for scenic and slightly cheesy drives around town.

Suddenly, I knew exactly what would be my salvation. I hadn't worked for Choca long but I knew his Achilles' heel—he was cheap. A penny-pincher. A miser. Think Scrooge. Liver and peas.

I flagged down Rafi and said, "Come up to the disco tonight. Drinks are on the house. Invite all your friends and anyone else you run into."

As he high-fived me, I smiled to myself. Rafi knew everybody in town. And Israelis can't resist something for free.

That evening, I lined up the shot glasses on the polished bar, put on a Spinners tape, and activated the disco ball. Pin pricks of red, gold, and blue lights orbited around the parquet dance floor.

Drumming my fingers on the bar, I wondered if anyone was going to take me up on my offer when suddenly there was a draft of frigid air and a pack of young people tumbled in, shedding their ski parkas. Soon the place was jumping. I didn't even lift the bottle lip when I poured drinks, just swooshed it over the glasses, filling them up in a cascade of Johnnie Walker. When I poured the last golden drop from one bottle, I grabbed another from the stockpile in the back room.

I was having so much fun dancing and laughing and cavorting while pouring drinks nonstop that a twinge of regret hovered inside me—this might be my last, and only, night as Queen of the Disco.

When I showed up the next evening for work, I

expected Choca to greet me at the bar entrance with my passport and marching orders. No sign of him, but because I had extended the free drink policy indefinitely, there was a large crowd lined up to enter the club.

Overnight, the club had become the most popular nightlife spot in the canton. Some of the fur-coat-clad partiers I was handing drinks to looked rather movie-star-ish. Apparently jetsetters liked free drinks, too!

Choca finally made an appearance a few nights later wearing an ill-fitting shiny polyester suit, his chest puffed up like a banty rooster's. He had brought an entourage of friends—all of whom looked like they belonged in the Mafia—to show off his star-studded, glamorous clientele.

By now, the disco was stuffed to the gills with a weird hodgepodge of seasonal workers rubbing shoulders with rich international boarding school brats, and the likes of Mick Jagger, Timothy Leary, high-cheekboned super-models, and pro skiers, all elbowing up to the bar and twirling on the dance floor.

Add to this the Grand Prix race car drivers who were in town for the internationally renowned Ollon-Villars hill climb, and it was a *Vogue* magazine wet dream.

My nightly blistering-cold thirty-minute walk home was cut down to five minutes when the famous race car drivers took turns giving me lifts back to the dorm after closing time. One night it would be an Italian in a Ferrari, the next a Brit in an Aston Martin. All gentlemen who gallantly opened the door of their fancy, super-sonic cars that sat one inch above the icy tarmac. They'd buckle me in, the engine would roar to life, and in a blurry streak I'd find myself down the mountain delivered to my doorstep with a kiss on the cheek and a *"Bonne nuit!"* before they zoomed off into the pre-dawn night.

Oddly, Choca left me alone but showed up every evening with his posse. It seemed his ego was willing to pay the alcohol bill in exchange for popularity. His group would sit at a table far off in a dark corner and leer at all the mini-skirted babes on the dance floor. He was the only one I had to deliver drinks to and, of course, there was no *pourboire*. He never said a word about the new free-drink policy.

I did finally get a gratuity. Jackie Stewart, the Grand Prix world champion nicknamed the "Flying Scot," passed me a dollar bill across the bar when I served him his drink. As he did so, he said in a thick Scottish brogue, "Thank ye, lassie. You're a fine dancer."

I was having a ball but working fourteen hours a day *and* partying was taking its toll. One particularly bustling evening, in an exhausted daze, I rushed from behind the bar and through the door with a tray of drinks to serve Choca. I was wearing my apricot silk gypsy blouse that I had had custom-designed in Paris for $20. The long bell sleeves fluttered and caught on the door handle, bringing me to an abrupt halt, but the drinks continued their trajectory through the air in a free fall. As I watched in horror, the glasses and their contents splashed across the laps of the brutish men sitting with Choca.

I was terrified yet relieved. Maybe now I would finally be released from this wheel of work captivity, but no. Choca, miraculously unscathed by the flood, pointed and laughed at his soaked friends.

Then, one morning, a week later, I awoke in a stark-white hospital room with a bandage around my head, tortured with a blazing headache.

Confused, not recognizing my surroundings, I drifted off in a hazy slumber. The next time I woke up, there was a nurse fiddling with the IV tubes sticking out of my arm.

"What is your name?" she softly asked in French-accented English. "Are you American?"

"What am I doing here?" I asked.

"One of your lodging mates carried you here late last night. She found you unconscious on the bathroom floor. You have anemia and a concussion. Do you remember passing out?"

"Not at all," I said.

Incredulous, I then asked, "The short, mean, ugly girl carried me here?"

The nurse laughed and said, "No. She was tall, strong, nice, and Spanish. She didn't know your name."

She felt my pulse and added, "You also appear to be suffering from mild starvation and dehydration."

I was so bone-tired and achy that what she said meant nothing. The clean bed and warm, quiet room lulled me back to sleep. The next time I opened my eyes, a policeman was standing at the foot of my bed holding a notepad.

He smiled kindly and asked in clipped English, "*Mademoiselle*, we are very concerned that you are so malnourished. Who is responsible for this and why have you not your passport or any identification?"

"Good question!" I said, and then filled him in on who had my passport and why.

The next day, I was still hooked up to the IV drip but felt much more myself. Rafi and some of my other friends

I'd made at the disco had stopped by to visit. They really missed me and the free drinks. They all agreed Choca was an ass but probably missed me too, as the club had been empty since my accident.

Rafi said, "And guess who is the new barmaid?"

"No, not the troll!"

He was laughing so hard he could only nod. He asked me what I was going to do next, and when he saw a copy of *Exodus* by Leon Uris on my bedside table, he told me about an airline that sold a cheap flight from Zurich to Tel Aviv. The book had ignited an overwhelming desire to go to Israel, and my mind began to race with the idea.

Two days later, I was getting antsy. The nurse had removed the bandage from around my head and the IV tubes from my arm and affirmed that the doctor was ready to discharge me. There was only one minor detail left, which was resolved when Choca suddenly strode into my hospital room, tossed my passport onto the bed, and said, "You're fired!"

As he turned and walked toward the door, I said sweetly, "Aren't you going to pay me my salary? I could ask the police to collect it for me if you are too busy right now."

He froze, spun around, and glowered. Rustling in his coat pocket, he pulled out a wallet and counted out 1200 Swiss francs.

Just the right amount to get me the student airfare that Rafi had told me about, with money to spare for my next adventure.

As I made my way to the main road just outside Villars to hitch a ride to Zurich, images of parting seas,

Bedouin tribes, and desert crossings in my mind, I passed Choca's bar and fingered the thick bundle of francs in my pocket, humming a Spinners song.

# FISH TRADER RAY

The Amazon 1974

*"Sitten ze down!"*

The German's livid face was as red as an equatorial sun setting through the pollution haze of a Third World metropolis.

Flora and I looked at each other. She winked and we wobbled the canoe back and forth with our newly acquired hip-shaking samba dance moves. Again. It was too delicious to be exacting revenge on the pissy photographer, who was tightly gripping both sides of the pencil-thin canoe. Murky, chocolate-brown river water splashed into the hull. This sent him into full-throttle hysteria.

*Should we tip him overboard?* I could tell Flora was thinking the same thing. No one would know. We were in the heart of the Upper Amazon Basin on a remote, flooded tributary.

He had shown up the day before. Ray had sent him. A photographer on assignment for a travel magazine. He had a lot of expensive camera gear with him.

Ray had also sent me to stay with Flora. I had arrived one week ago with a hammock that I hung from the rafters of her tiny hut. We'd hit it off, having more in common than one would suspect between a tribal Amazonian woman and a middle-class California chick. We were the same age and had the same men issues. Daily I went out on the river with her three young children to catch live fish in handheld nets. We would carefully flip the iridescent wriggling fish from the netting into tightly woven, waterproof baskets. Flora sent these to Ray via the weekly mail *panga*—a long, narrow, motorized canoe. Ray was a tropical fish trader.

It was a two-day boat ride from the jungle port town of Leticia, where I had come from, to Flora's hut. I had wanted to spend time deep in the Amazon Basin. That meant getting off the well-trafficked thoroughfare of the Amazon River and into its backwaters.

Fish Trader Ray was the man for my Amazon plan.

I had met Ray in a hotel lobby in Bogotá, Colombia at the beginning of my South American odyssey four months earlier. Fantasies of rubbing shoulders with a bunch of colorful characters straight out of Graham Greene and Gabriel García Márquez novels was the extent of my travel plans. And of course, to experience the Amazon and go to Carnival.

I landed in Bogotá on a $125 round trip ticket on Avianca Airlines from Miami. I spoke zero Spanish but managed to find a dingy yet elegant hotel with high ceilings, fans, and gleaming hardwood floors in the colonial part of town. I was immediately enthralled by the mustachioed men with battered leather briefcases drinking *café tinto* holding their business meetings in the overstuffed lobby chairs, and the plain-faced Catholic nuns from missions deep in the *selva* sipping from green glass Coca-Cola bottles. Then there was Ray—a big, loud twangy-talking Texan, who looked like he desperately needed something cool to drink, wearing a pastel striped shirt with sweat stains under his armpits.

Desi Arnaz and Carmen Miranda were my only window into Latin culture. Oh, and the crazy nonstop partying Brazilians I had met the year before in Paris. Expecting salsa and rumba dancing in the streets with sexy ladies crowned in tropical fruit hats, I was dismayed to find Bogotá a slummy and polluted place populated by sullen citizens shuffling down the sidewalks. At 8,600 feet in elevation, this dreary city was chilly and overcast with *nada* a Busby Berkeley fruit hat in sight.

It had been a frustrating arrival and I was piqued.

After checking in I wandered into the streets to find my first local meal. There were no restaurants, just a few hole-in-the-wall stores in this rundown part of town. A gang of young Colombian toughs in flared jeans were milling about on the corner, eying me. The soundtrack from *West Side Story* played in my head: "When you're a Jet you're a Jet all the way, from your first cigarette to your last dying day."

Gulp. Chin up. I crossed the street toward them. "*Hola*" I said with false bravado, making hand gestures to indicate I was looking for food. They were as surprised as I was by my forthrightness. Surrounding me like a military escort, they marched me to a stairwell leading down to a dive with six tables. In unison they poked their heads into the place and yelled, "*Abuela!*" A darling grey-haired woman about half my height appeared from behind a beaded curtain, gave me a welcoming smile, and gestured for me to sit at one of the plastic flower-print-covered tables. The gang departed, but not before they all kissed their grandma on both cheeks and formally shook my hand. The woman handed me a menu and I recognized one of the items offered: *tostadas*.

"I'll have an order of that," I said.

Savory smells emanated from the tiny kitchen. The short señora shuffled out from behind the clacking curtains and set a small plate of plain toast in front of me. Where were the tortillas, meat, cheese, guacamole, topped with sour cream?

I had just learned my first gustatory word in Spanish. *Tostada*=toast.

With two pieces of toast in my grumbling belly, I headed back to the hotel tired, grumpy, and ready for a hot shower and a long nap. I turned the water on full blast and within minutes the small bathroom steamed like a sauna. As I stepped into the shower stall, a strange gurgling sound grabbed my attention. Peering through the mist I was horrified to see a waterfall gushing out of the toilet onto the bathroom tile and out the door in a steady rush across the mahogany bedroom floor. No matter how many towels I threw down to block the flow, it was unstoppable. Without thinking, I wrapped the last towel around me, scampered out of the room and down the grand staircase to the reception desk.

The clerk was shocked that I was standing at the counter sporting only a bath towel. "Americans can be *so* inappropriate and *such* attention-getters," I'm sure he was thinking as he tried not to look me up and down. My bosom was barely covered as I fluttered my hands and flapped my arms to communicate that there was an imminent disaster happening upstairs. "A flood! The toilet! Hurry! In my room!" I squawked like a parrot.

I now had the full attention of the clerk and everyone in the lobby. But nobody understood. The urgency was completely lost on them, yet they certainly found me amusing. They laughed as I continued to gesticulate that there was a serious problem and it was not me dressed only in a towel.

The sound of splashing water got them to focus. A river of water cascaded down each stair like a liquid Slinky. *Now* they were looking at something besides me.

I slumped in one of those overstuffed chairs in the lobby, completely ignored, and waited for them to fix the toilet and mop up the mess.

"Looks like a rough day, young lady." The large bulk of the man with the stained shirt I had seen earlier stood above me with a concerned look on his face, his thinning sandy-grey hair slicked back in an impressive helmet. "I'm Ray Johnson and you obviously don't speak Spanish. Can I help you?"

He didn't seem lecherous and reminded me of a mix of Sean Connery and Santa Claus, so I hiked my towel up a little higher and confided, "This is my first day here. Where can I get a good meal?"

"The hotel restaurant has quite decent fare. May I take a fella American to dinner? Not now, of course..."

I giggled, relieved to be speaking English, and tugged at the towel again in a futile attempt to cover an inch more of my legs, self-conscious about how I must seem wrapped only in a towel.

The hotel staff moved me to a drier room, where I lingered in a luxuriously hot and uneventful shower. I gussied up in a new pair of jeans and a crisp, cream-colored linen blouse, and met Ray in the dining room. A waiter with a white napkin draped over his arm took our order. Ray counseled, "Colombian food can be very starchy and bland. They cook with a lot of yucca, which has the texture of a stringy potato without flavor. They also add fistfuls of cilantro to every dish. Try the *carne asada* with a hearts of palm salad. Have a beer, Argentinean Malbec, or a Chilean cabernet, if you like, but I don't drink."

"What are you doing in Bogotá?" I asked after we had ordered and I sipped on a lush, garnet-hued cabernet.

"I'm a tropical fish trader, along with other commodities, and I'm here to drum up buyers."

I nodded as a waiter bustled by with a fragrant, steaming dish. I could smell the cilantro. My stomach rumbled.

"Why are you in Bogotá?" he asked.

"This was the cheapest airfare destination I could find to South America. I'll be traveling for a year or two."

"So where are you going on your South American grand tour?" Ray asked with a grandfatherly twinkle in his milky sea-blue eyes.

"The novel *Green Mansions* inspired me to travel the waterways of the Amazon Basin and explore its green veil. I also really want to go to Carnival in Bahia, Brazil and samba dance in the streets. I think the cheapest way to get there might be down the Amazon River."

He thought this was hysterical and laughed till he wiped tears from his eyes but finally responded, "You might be right, but do you know how long the river is or where you are going to launch?"

I answered seriously, "It's two thousand miles to Belém in Brazil and I'm going in via the headwaters of the Rio Napo in Ecuador, just like the Spanish explorer and conquistador Francisco de Orellana did in 1542. Orellana's voyages served as partial influence for the Werner Herzog's film *Aguirre, the Wrath of God*. I've done my research."

He tried to stop grinning and said, "Well, you must come visit me on your way to Brazil. Leticia is a trading outpost in Colombia on the Amazon River bordered by Peru and Brazil. I live there with my common-law Yagua wife, who's from the Red Macaw clan, and our passel of kids."

He seemed sort of old to have a young family, but I kept that thought to myself. The waiter brought our dishes. The savory aroma of grilled rare meat was irresistible. Silence reigned for a few moments as we both ceremoniously picked up our silver-inlaid steak knives and dug in eagerly.

"How did you end up in the Amazon?" I stopped chewing long enough to ask.

Ray waggled his fork at me and said, "In the 1950s I

was a photographer for *National Geographic*. We were down here making a film when our plane crashed in the jungle. Everyone survived, but I got malaria and was too ill to continue on with the film crew. Besides, I fell in love, several times, and stayed in Leticia. Been there twenty-one years."

"That's about when I was born," I said.

He chuckled and carved into his blood-red steak while still talking. "Thought I could discover an unknown tribe and make a name for myself by filming them. I'd canoe far up the rivers and ask around, hear rumors about tribes that were still virgin to the white man's eyes. I even encountered an isolated clan up near the Orinoco River delta on the Venezuelan border. They didn't cook me and even initiated me into one of their hunting trip rituals where they blew snuff up my nose with a blowgun. It knocked me out for hours, and terrifying giant anacondas and toothy, yowling jaguars populated my hallucinations. Oh, and I threw up. A lot."

Mouth gaping open, I stared and asked in disbelief, "You took psychedelic drugs with a cannibalistic tribe?"

He shrugged and said, "I didn't know. Thought it was cocaine or something, though the blowgun was a lot longer than a straw or a rolled-up dollar bill. I was in-like-flint after that experience and slept in the chief's hut, completely convinced I had found *the* lost tribe until one night, swinging in my hammock, I noticed light glinting off a Coca-Cola bottle hanging high up in the rafters. Boy, was I disappointed!"

"After that, I started taking tourists and scientists into the jungle since I knew it so well. Funny things happened.

One lady botanist was terrified of piranha and continually obsessed about them. I reassured her they were not in the middle of the river we were traveling on but schooled in the eddies along the bank. Right then, we hit a wake and a piranha flew from the water, arced into the boat, and landed on her head, latching itself onto her forehead. Getting that fish off was one of the biggest challenges of my life. I didn't know whether to laugh or cry as I pried the piranha's pointy teeth apart. She made me deaf with her screaming. Fortunately, it was a flesh wound. The fish didn't take a big bite since there's not a lot of skin to bite into on the forehead."

"Ray, that's impossible!" I laughed.

He shook his head and said, "You wouldn't believe how weird it can get in the Amazon."

He continued, "At that point I decided it was too difficult being a tour guide, so I put the word out among the various indigenous tribes that came to Leticia for supplies that I was buying exotic birds like macaws, toucans, and Amazon parrots. There was a big market in the States, but that ended when so many died in quarantine because of avian diseases. And you couldn't sneak 'em in anymore after customs officials upped their security checks because of the escalating drug traffic out of South America. So now, I do fish."

Several months later, having mastered Spanish out of sheer necessity since my flummoxed first night in Bogotá, I was still tenaciously heading by boat to Carnival in Brazil.

Traders' canoes languidly ferried me down the Rio Napo in Ecuador to Iquitos, Peru where the Napo flowed into the two-mile-wide Amazon River.

One sweltering day I found myself scrambling up a muddy embankment to the dock leading into Leticia. Ray's invitation to visit was not forgotten. I hoped he would introduce me to the "real" Amazon.

The early morning sun was already blazing on the Amazonian frontier town as I walked the wooden sidewalk that went back toward Leticia. Electric Blue Morpho butterflies burst from the rain puddles while mangy mongrels skulked about, picking at piles of fish bones haloed in clouds of botflies. Indians in feathered headdresses and ear plugs, their skin painted in red *achiote*, hustled past on their way to the open-air market, carrying spider monkeys, black caiman, emerald-green macaws, and even a terrified hissing jaguar kitten, trussed on poles or trapped in basket cages swinging from the Indians' blowguns. One shirtless *mestizo* in ragged soccer shorts had a twelve-foot anaconda draped around his shoulders. He caught sight of me and before I could wave him off, he wrapped the snake around my neck, holding onto the back of its head so it couldn't bite, and asked for money for a photo. The reptile was uncomfortably weighty and smelled of snake urine, which has its own distinctly unpleasant pungent odor. As I looked at its skin, I noticed ticks bloating out from underneath its scales. Repulsed, I wiggled out of the snake's tightening grip. Bursts of gunfire, coming from a ramshackle bar perched on stilts overhanging the river, punctuated the cacophony at the dock. This roughshod town assaulted all of my senses at once, invoking Hieronymus Bosch's paintings of hell.

Salty sweat poured down my face, stinging my eyes. I managed to make my way to the deserted main plaza and sat, panting, on a bench under the pathetic shade of a scrawny palm tree. Scratching under my shirt, concerned one of the ticks had hopped off the snake for a warmer host, I wondered how to find Ray. He didn't have a phone or an address, and had simply told me, "When you get to Leticia, just ask for Fish Trader Ray."

I motioned to a young boy kicking a ball across the otherwise-empty plaza. "*Dónde está* Fish Trader Ray?"

The boy looked puzzled and then asked, "*Pescadero Raymundo?*"

He motioned for me to stay where I was, and ran off down a side street. Minutes later, Ray appeared on an exhaust-spewing motorcycle with his wife and several kids hanging off his wide girth like a bunch of ripe bananas.

Ray hesitantly greeted me, but then a huge smile broke across his face and he embraced me in a sweaty bear hug, introducing me to his family. He said, "You found me. I almost didn't recognize you. You've lost a lot of weight since we met in Bogotá and your clothes are pretty beat up. Still going to Carnival?"

We all sipped Coca-Colas at an outdoor café, the kids playing with a giant ebony rhinoceros beetle that scuttled in the dirt under our table. The frosty, curvaceous bottle in my hand yielded the most delicious, sugary-sweet, icy-cold soft drink I had ever quaffed. Surprised that he had paid for our drinks in dollars, I asked him why, and he explained, "The dollar is more common than pesos because of the drug cartels coming through here to the

States. Leticia is a hub for outlaws, contraband, and cocaine."

Ray entertained me by pointing out CIA agents trying to blend in as American businessmen in dark suits, their bulging necks and biceps giving them away.

"Why are they in this godforsaken place?" I asked.

He raised his eyebrows and talked out of the side of his mouth in a whisper. "You don't want to know. They protect the drug trade and make sure the government officials are cooperating."

"My tax money is paying for *that*?"

This further heightened my desire to get out of town pronto and return to the green tangle of the jungle. Give me poisonous bugs, blood-sucking bats, carnivorous fish, and strangling snakes anytime over men with guns.

"Ray, I *really* don't want to stay here. I'd love to spend time with you and your family but this place scares me. Do you have any suggestions for how I might get farther into the backwaters of the Amazon? I want to see the rarer flora and fauna, and then head toward Brazil and Carnival. I've been practicing my samba steps…"

He nodded sympathetically and said, "Leticia is a very dangerous place. There's a mail boat traveling downriver leaving late this afternoon. My buddy Marco, the captain, will drop you off at Flora's, about a two-day boat ride from here on one of the more obscure branches of the Japurá. She collects exotic aquarium fish for me and welcomes visitors."

Ray walked back down to the wharf and got me settled into Marco's twenty-foot-long *panga*. He waved goodbye with his weather-worn Panama hat, surrounded by his retinue of barefoot children and his short, stoic, native wife. Another gunshot emanated from the stilt bar, as if a starting pistol was announcing our departure. Leticia quickly—and thankfully—faded into the distance. That town was no place for a young woman—unless she was plying her trade.

The sunset across the twenty-mile expanse of the Amazon River was a fantastical light show of tangerine spectral colors. The sultry water's surface shimmered in a coppery-peach glow. I curled up on a lumpy sack of mail, appreciating the tranquility, and dreamily watched as the constellation of the Southern Cross faintly appeared in the gloaming of twilight.

We chugged along the sluggish waters of the Amazon River with dozens of other craft, from slipper-size dugouts paddled by plumage-bedecked natives to rusty cargo container ships struggling upstream to Iquitos or Pucallpa. My only company in the stern of the boat were a wild peccary in a slat cage who, thankfully, gave up squealing after a few hours, and Marco's pet capuchin monkey, who made a game out of looking for nits on my scalp. His gentle preening soothed me during the hazy, heat-baked day. I had to lie on my pack, as the mischievous monkey also enjoyed digging through it with his dexterous digits— squeezing out the toothpaste or chewing on the soap bar. His most naughty and annoying trick was absconding with my silky underwear, placing it on his head like a beret and keeping just out of my grasp. We shared a passion for cashews and boiled palm nuts that I cut up and fed to him. He was too cute to be mad at for very long especially when he innocently batted his coal-black eyelashes at me.

Toward the end of the second day we detoured up a coffee-colored river confluence and into narrower tributaries, finally arriving at a small hut on stilts above the riparian jungle terrain.

There was no terra firma to disembark on, so we motored right up to the porch railing. Marco introduced me to a compact, smiling woman with bright white teeth, mocha-toned skin, and peculiar pale green-blue eyes that flashed an invitation of friendship. Flora reached down, gave me her calloused hand, and hauled me up from the boat's rim into her twelve-square-foot thatched-roof shack. Marco confirmed he would come get me in a week and hook me up with a ride to Manaus midway between Leticia and the mouth of the Amazon River in Belém, where a bus would provide transport to Bahia in about three days. "Just in time for Carnival!" he emphasized as he shoved off, in a hurry to get back to the main river branch and visit his family. The monkey screeched goodbye with a furrowed brow as he watched me, and my pack contents, fade into the dusk. He was wearing something on his head...

Flora seemed pleased to have me as a guest. She was isolated here with just her three young children, all under age five, for company—her only social life the occasional visitor Ray sent or the infrequent passing trader. The tribe she came from lived much farther upriver and she never saw them. I never asked why she lived by herself, but I got the impression she was an outcast due to her mixed blood.

She spoke passable Spanish so we communicated easily. I agreed to contribute to the food kitty and also help her with household chores, fishing, foraging, and childcare.

When we weren't out fishing we cooked, swept, wove baskets, and lounged in the hammocks, sharing stories and braiding my hair. The kids were fascinated by my back-length blond tresses and fooled with them constantly. I teased that they should open a beauty salon. This sent them into giggle-fits, as Flora and I were the only women for many miles in this riverine no-man's-land.

Flora's tipsy canoe was the only way to get around. Carved out of a single tree trunk, it floated just a half-inch above the waterline. Balance was essential when we sat, stood, or paddled.

At night, after the children were asleep, we'd slip into the dugout with flashlights and glide silently into the lagoons surrounding the shack, looking for black caiman. Their eyes glowed a spooky citrine-green in the distance like iridescent marbles hovering right above the obsidian-dark waters. We'd quickly shine the flashlight into their eyes to mesmerize them before they disappeared below the surface. Then we'd paddle over and gently tap on their prehistoric boney heads. This would break the spell and, *plop*, they'd sink underneath the inky water.

That was about it for nightly entertainment.

My visions of the magical realm of the jungle that *Green Mansions* had stimulated were real. How glorious the gigantic, two meters in diameter, Reina Victoria lily pads were—each one a universe inhabited by jade-green frogs and giant-legged bugs—and how strange and mythical the pink river dolphins appeared, quietly rising up and sinking back into the muddy malachite waters as our canoe wove through the mesh curtain of vines and drifting roots. I was finally living the fantasy that had inspired the long and arduous journey I'd taken to get here. Traveling through Flora's watery world was worth every bug bite and petrifyingly scary moment.

Over her brazier set on the floorboards, we shared meals of smoked monkey stew, boiled palm nuts, dried pirarucu—the largest freshwater fish in the world, and my favorite: grilled capybara—the world's biggest rodent. We also did what women do all around the globe—we talked about men. Ironically, she had the same boyfriend problems I did. We were both attracted to the irresponsible, adventurous types—dark handsome guys who sported toned bodies and flaunted irrepressible smiles that could melt instantly into a silent, sullen restlessness. Hers was a bigger dilemma, as she also seemed to get pregnant and have children with the various Casanova traders and explorers who canoed past.

The week at Flora's passed quickly. I was ready to travel onward to Carnival, especially once the sour German arrived the day before I was to leave, and put a crimp in our fun factor. He took up half the hut with his camera gear and shoveled all the stew onto his plate leaving a thigh bone and some sauce for the rest of us. He spoke in a bullying baronial tone of self-importance ordering us about like servants, but Flora needed the money he was paying for her guide services, so I couldn't shove him over the railing and feed him to the caiman like I wanted to. Thankfully, Marco showed up when promised and had consigned a boat ride to Manaus for me. I hugged her wild, spunky kids goodbye and promised Flora I would stay in touch with her via Ray and return to visit her special watery world someday—maybe with my own future children in tow.

I did arrive in Bahia on the first day of Carnival as Marco predicted, and danced nonstop in the streets for a week. Several pair of shoes were worn out as I tried to keep up with the battery of booty-shaking, sexy samba mamas who paraded around town 24/7 in their stilettos, towering headdresses, skimpy costumes, and mile-wide electric smiles. Shimmy, shimmy, smile, rotate, wave to the crowd; then run, run, run to catch up with the frenzied drum bands on the motorized parade floats and shimmy some more. It reminded me of the moves Flora taught me to prepare me for Carnival, standing up in her tipsy canoe, scaring that silly photographer. Shimmy, shimmy, shake, shake, giggle, guffaw! Sisterhood discovered deep in the Amazon.

The Amazon and Carnival faded into a blur of further larger-than-life adventures traversing Iguaçu Falls and the glaciers of Patagonia, over the Atacama Desert to Bolivia, and months later, flying home from Ecuador—a full circle from where I began my Amazonian quest.

I went back to California and started an import business. For seven years I commuted to South America, and whenever I could find a flight from Colombia or Peru to Leticia, I'd take a detour and visit my friend Ray and his growing family. Leticia held a certain backwater charming seediness that grew on me the more I explored the region. Flora had married one of her Casanova's and moved to Iquitos and I never saw her again.

The last time I saw Ray was thirty years ago, right

before I sold my import company. He was hoisting me into the cargo hull of an un-pressurized plane on a dirt runway filled to the gills with odoriferous planks of salted pirarucu fish. Throngs of Indians pushed and shoved to get on the plane that provided the only transport to Bogotá on a random schedule. Luckily, they were much more diminutive than Ray, who tossed me like a football, launching me over the indigenous feathery finery and headfirst onto stacks of smelly fish. As the plane sputtered and the propellers whirred, we lifted upward. There was Ray on the runway below, large and pasty-white, enthusiastically waving his sweat-stained Ecuadorian Panama hat, grinning and squinting upward toward the blazing orb of the sun. His kids taller, his wife shorter. Fish Trader Ray. My Amazon man. Straight out of a novel.

# MUTINY IN THE GALÁPAGOS

Ecuador 1975

After a few hours of reconnoitering the dusty streets of Puerto Ayora, I found a fisherman who would take two off-duty scientific researchers and me on a tour of the Galápagos Islands if we paid for his beer and gas. We handed him a wad of crumpled bank notes, threw our rucksacks onto his smelly rust bucket of a boat, and headed out to sea. I was feeling quite proud of myself for activating a plan of exploration so expediently, having only just arrived on the island of Santa Cruz that morning.

*Chug, cough, sputter. Chug, cough, sputter.* The boat determinedly plowed through the watery troughs in spite of its congested rhythm, diesel fumes in our wake. Bound for islands unknown, I had a smile on my face, until I noticed we were headed straight for a gargantuan rock. The captain was nowhere in sight. Alarmed, I tripped down the steps leading to the dark, dank hold to find him passed out on a mattress, his rumbling snores reverberating throughout the cabin. I shook him until his bloodshot eyes creaked open. He stared at me crossed-eyed, then belched in my face. Judging by the plethora of empty cans strewn around him, he had stealthily managed to consume an entire case of beer in less than thirty minutes. Luckily, one of the scientists knew how to take control of the boat. Disappointed, we turned the hulk around and headed back to port without hitting anything along the way. This was my first mutiny.

Short of cash and bankrupt of a game plan, I abandoned the alcoholic captain and my fellow mutineers. At least no one had died. I couldn't say the same thing about the train trip I had taken two weeks earlier. I was riding on the roof (standard seating on overcrowded trains in South America) of the 1800s narrow-gauge steam locomotive that connected Quito, the mountainous Andean capitol of Ecuador, with the port town of Quayaquil via the dramatic Avenue of the Volcanoes. I always chose the roof to avoid the crowded, stinky conditions inside and get a spectacular view with thrills provided around every leaning turn. The train shunted back and forth along the steep, rocky promontory appropriately named *Nariz del Diablo* (the Devil's Nose), and suddenly came to a grinding halt. An Otavalan Indian had tumbled off on one of the curves. There he lay on the tracks—at least part of him. His head had rolled into the weeds a few feet away.

Feeling depressed and exhausted over my grim and graphic train odyssey, too many sweaty nights in sleazy bordellos waiting for transport, and the failed launch with the drunken fisherman into the wondrous world of rare endemic creatures, I craved chocolate.

The only store in tiny Puerto Ayora was a dimly-lit shack stocked with *cerveza*, *cigarillos*, and *Manichos*. Standing in line, the Manicho candy bar already unwrapped and melting in my mouth, I looked over the shoulder of the imposing shirtless man in front of me who was taking way too much time. He was writing a check. A check! There were no banks in the Galápagos. His robust curlicue signature spelled out *Freddy Schmidt*.

I'd read about the legendary Schmidts in a book lent to me by my scientist seatmates in the drafty military supply plane flying from Guayaquil to the Galápagos. Being young, blond, persistent, *and* female are great qualities to possess if you need a ride somewhere. Just as I had been about to give up completely on finding a way to cross the five hundred miles of Pacific Ocean that separated the Galápagos from mainland Ecuador, a pilot offered me a lift in the camouflage-painted DC-3 to Seymour Field on the island of Baltra. The scientists were going out to the Darwin Research Center to study the reluctant procreation tactics of Lonesome George, the last remaining giant tortoise of his kind. Or maybe find him another tortoise femme fatale from a neighboring island who would stimulate his libido.

The book informed me that in the 1600s, the Galápagos was a stop for the Spanish galleons on their way from Central America back to Spain with their absconded booty. One of the reasons Lonesome George didn't have a lot of dating prospects was the passing seafarers (otherwise known as pirates) had stuffed the tortoises into the hold as a living food source. Another detail of interest in the book was about one of the first European settlers on the Galápagos—a larger-than-life character named Reinhart Schmidt, who still lived there in a cave. The hulking man standing in line in front of me might be one of the founding fathers, the original settlers of the Galápagos. Or their unshaven son.

I reached up and tapped this Schmidt fellow on the shoulder. "Can I buy you a Manicho?" I said with feigned innocence.

He turned slowly, sized me up as if I had antennas, then responded in a booming, shack-shaking American voice, "You bet!"

I gathered up a fistful of candy bars and followed him into the glaring midday sun. We sat on a nearby fishing pier and introduced ourselves. Freddy Schmidt seemed to like Manichos as much as I did. I think he also liked blonds.

We lounged on the splintered planks, slowly licking off the chocolate dripping from the wrappers. I asked, "Are you related to Reinhart Schmidt?"

"Yeah, he's my dad. Sailed a boat here from Europe with his brothers. Said he was leaving because of Hitler."

He asked, "Where are you from?"

"San Franciscan, fourth generation; my relatives arrived during the Gold Rush."

"So you're a hippie?" he asked with a smirk.

I didn't answer, and after awhile Freddy asked, "Would you like to meet my wife? She's American and really misses her friends and hamburgers. We're on our honeymoon."

We hopped into a small dinghy tied to the pier and he rowed us out to a sailboat anchored in the bay. Draped on the bow was a tanned bleach-blond babe in a shell-pink bikini.

Freddy yelled up at her, "Catch the line—we have a visitor from California." She leaned forward, offering me her hand. I grabbed it and she pulled me aboard past her ample and obviously-enhanced bosom swinging like ripe cantaloupes. "My name is Sally Ann," she said in a Southern drawl. Her teeth gleamed. She seemed thrilled to meet me. "Freddy and I met in Florida. We just got married and he wants to show me where he grew up so he built this boat and we sailed here through the Panama Canal, arriving just the other day."

It was an odd pleasure to be in the company of Americans and be completely understood for the first time in months. Sally Ann told me all about her life in the States. "I have a little white poodle named Lollipop. He stayed with my mom. Freddy said I couldn't bring him because he would be shark bait." She kept her eyes down when she spoke and talked in breathless run-on sentences.

Freddy was pleased with our chatty connection and interjected, "I want to show my little wife the secrets of the Galápagos and my favorite boyhood haunts. We're going to visit the pupping fur seals and my penguin buddies. Would you like to come along with us?"

Yes! This was why I had waited weeks in Guayaquil for the supply boat to be fixed (which it never was). This was why I had stayed in that dingy whorehouse serenaded by grunts and moans, itchy from sweat and bed bugs.

That Manicho I bought Freddy was turning out to be the best ten-cent investment I'd ever made.

At 21 I was naïve, and more enthusiastic than smart. I failed to consider that it was a little weird for him to invite me on their honeymoon and that he hadn't consulted with his beloved. I bit the hook of a serendipitous once-in-a-lifetime opportunity to be steeped in the insider's secrets of Darwin's Petri dish.

Nodding like a bobblehead doll, I asked, "What can I do in exchange for this generous offer?"

"How about you cook for us? Sally Ann doesn't know how."

It turned out Sally Ann didn't know how to do much except work on her tan, but there was something sweet and sincere about her that I liked.

"I love to cook. When do you want to leave?"

"We'll buy supplies and leave tomorrow after Reinhart's birthday party."

I was extremely relieved to have free passage to the wild island kingdoms—each of the twenty-one rocky dots of land a haven to exclusive species that had made Darwin salivate. Back in the early 1970s, it was not easy getting to the Galápagos, as proven by my several failed attempts. There were no tours or tourists. For me, it was part of a two-year solo wander-about in South America discovering the romantically epic and remote places I'd only read about in explorer books: the Amazon, Patagonia, Tierra Del Fuego, and of course, the Galápagos.

We rowed back to the pier, tied up the dinghy, and returned to the same tiny store where we met. He stocked up on flour-sack bags stuffed with carrots, onions, and potatoes.

I scripted gourmet menus in my head and asked, "Are we going to get any other food supplies?"

Freddy looked at me and said impatiently, "No, this is all they have, but we'll troll for tuna."

It appeared that my assigned job was not going to be very demanding, so I filed the recipes for mushroom cream sauce, conk with a Tahitian lime marinade, and gazpacho back in my mental cookbook.

After stowing away our supplies and stuffing my rucksack under the folding dining table, we hopped back into the tipsy dinghy and headed to shore for the birthday festivities.

Laughter, strumming guitars, and tinkling glasses serenaded us as we walked the short distance to Reinhart's abode past driftwood fishing shacks and cinderblock huts, prickly pear cacti and thorny acacias. Candles lit the way along a stone path. As we approached the yawning cave entrance that Reinhart had carved out of the hillside, a barefoot man wearing only tattered swim trunks strode toward us. Freddy winced as he was clapped hard on the back and Sally Ann got a very long squeeze. Reinhart eyed me up and down and then gave me a bear hug, too.

Was he 50, 60, 70? It was difficult to discern his age as he had a permanently grizzled caveman look with long, untrimmed silvery hair, a muscular body coated in a Naugahyde tan, and fiery blue eyes.

Guests milled around the rocky entrance—mostly researchers from the Darwin Station. I recognized my two compatriots from our aborted fishing boat mission.

Grabbing my elbow, Reinhart swept me into his lair

and filled an empty mayonnaise jar with white lightning. "Drink up! I bet you've never had this stuff before. It will set you on fire. I make it myself and also light the lamps with it," he said with a wink and concussive back slap that almost knocked me over.

I tippled the clear liquid with a strong odor that made my eyes water and looked around at the hand-carved furniture, random bones, frayed sepia photos, seal and goat skulls, giant tortoise shells, and other bric-a-brac reminiscent of the Smithsonian that adorned his cave.

Outside, unadulterated stars appeared in the blue-black velvet canvas of the night sky. We danced for hours under their approving twinkle.

Reinhart was right. That hooch was mind-bending. I did things that night I still don't remember but everyone else did.

The next morning as I crawled out from under a picnic table, Reinhart's face appeared in front of mine. A wild, lascivious look lit up his eyes as he raved, "You are some wild dancer! Balanced on a table, spun like a top, and didn't even break a leg."

Pungent alcohol-fumed breath gusted forth as he declared, "Let's have another party tonight! When's *your* birthday?"

I backed out of his cave into the glaring sun and hobbled to port, looking for Freddy and Sally Ann. They were eating a late breakfast in the living room of the only restaurant in town that was really just someone's house. A chicken ran between their legs as the proprietor chased it down with a cleaver. "Oh, look who's still alive!" they chorused, not meaning the chicken, who was destined for our plates.

As I gingerly sat down at their table, Freddy said, "You didn't tell us you were a pro dancer and party animal."

I held my forehead, moaned, and said, "That *really* was not me. I was possessed by the firewater gods."

The signora had caught the chicken and after a while, we could hear it sputtering in the frying pan. Later, we tried to eat it. It was so tough from being an Olympic marathon runner around the dining tables that all it was good for was a laugh as we bounced the rubbery drumsticks on the Formica table, looking rather like hungover children with rattles.

Later, back on the boat, the sound of heavy metal chains bouncing off the hull jarred me awake from a much-needed afternoon nap. I was still feeling queasy as Freddy raised the anchor.

Boning up on the islands that we were about to explore, I read in a tattered history book used to steady the table leg that during the early twentieth century, the islands were inhabited by very few settlers and were used as a penal colony, the last closing in 1959 when the islands were declared a national park.

Might I have just been partying with ex-members of the penal colony that had graduated to "settler" status, otherwise known as convicts? These were my contrary thoughts as I found myself sailing forth once again with strangers.

We swept out of the harbor with a stiff wind at our back.

Sally Ann and I lay on deck, watching the feathery

clouds sweep past overhead. Blearily I asked, "Where are we headed?"

Freddy's ropey arms hoisted the sails. "First stop? My penguin buddies on Isla Fernandina."

Freddy looked at me with a grin, probably still seeing me dancing on the table top. "Hey, bang a bottle on the prow and see if the dolphins show up."

As the bow cut through the lapis waves, I leaned over its edge and thudded an empty beer bottle on the side. *Thunk thunk thunk.* Mesmerized by the bubbly curl on the lacy crests, a shadowy torpedo shape appeared, darting below the sea's opaque surface. A sleek dorsal fin rose out of the water, and then a nose and the shining obsidian eyes of a bottlenose dolphin. Before I could yell back to Freddy that the bottle banging had worked, a pod arrived, leaping ahead of the boat. One by one, they swam into position inches from the boat hull. Swift and graceful, they choreographed their dance like an Ice Capades minuet in three-quarter time. Water sheeted off their compact steel-blue bodies. Pirouetting and spinning in joyous bounds, keeping ahead of the boat and grinning up at me, they were working really hard at having fun.

Realizing the sun was setting and distracted by mundane but demanding stomach growls, I asked, "What about the tuna? I should get dinner ready."

"No problem." Freddy threw a thick twenty-five-pound test fishing line with a wickedly barbed hook off the back of the boat.

I thought a lead-weighted hook with bait was supposed to sink, but the bait skipped along the ocean's surface because we were racing across the water so quickly. As I pondered when I should heat up the skillet, the line pulled taut and a silvery tuna bounced along the wave tops, twisting and turning, trying to unhook itself. Just as Freddy was showing me how to reel the three-foot-long fish into the boat, a massive shark burst out of the water and snagged the hook and fish whole, then jerked it under the sea in the blink of an eye.

This became a daily occurrence, and with it came a dilemma. It was easy catching a tuna; the challenge was reeling it in before the sharks nabbed it. And there were a lot of super-sized sharks in the Galápagos due to the abundance of food sources in the nutrient-rich Humboldt Current.

When we anchored in a bay to swim to shore (more fun than rowing and much more dangerous) to explore the wildlife there, one of us would be assigned to shark watch while the others swam swiftly to the beach. The sharks' fins could be seen circling far off, but the radius had to be several hundred feet before we felt safe enough to dive in and go for it. No time wasted dawdling or ogling, even if spotted eagle rays carpeted the sandy bottom. In one particularly crystalline bay, I was distracted by a school of translucent giant squid peering at me with luminous eyes. I circled above them but then heard Freddy shout from the boat, "Shark, shark! Get your ass to the beach!"

There was some karmic payback, though. We wanted to use the sharks for bait, but how would we catch them since they were too big to reel in on the tuna line? I had the answer—tampons! Two women whose menstrual cycles had synced after just a day of being in close quarters provided plenty of bait for catching tuna. We speared a bloody cotton tube to an ominously large hook and Freddy lowered it into the water.

Sharks are able to detect as little as one part per million of blood in seawater, so it didn't take long to attract hefty hammerheads and greedy whitetip reef sharks. It is thought that the shape of the hammerhead shark's head enhances olfaction, as the nostrils are spaced far apart. That might explain why there were so many of them churning the waters around the boat for a dinky tampon.

Leaning over the rail to watch the tampon sink downward in a watery pink halo, I stared in frozen horror into the giant, teeth-lined, gaping mouth that lunged upward. The tampon dangled far down in the dark precipice of its gullet. Most of the time we would just tease the sharks and pull the tampon up before they got hooked but when we needed meat for bait, Freddy would brazenly gaff the hammerhead with a huge steel barb and yank it over the rail in one mighty swoop. Sally Ann and I would jump back and hide behind the mast as the shark flailed on the deck. Freddy, in the stance of a gladiator about to slay his enemy, whacked the thrashing shark with a razor-sharp machete, severing its head. We had to be careful not to slip in the spattered blood and end up in the water bobbing like bait ourselves.

Over and over again, in morbid fascination, we watched these prehistoric monsters lunge from the sea toward our faces with only a handrail separating gnashing razor teeth from flesh. My entire head, neck, and shoulders would have fit in their mouths.

Every marine creature we encountered over the next

two weeks came in extra large. Manta rays were ten feet across; thirty-foot whale sharks blocked the view while we snorkeled; moray eels snaked by, free-swimming in sets of three, each one a moss-green six-foot-long ribbon flecked in gold.

Then there were the land animals, each super-sized species living on a different island. Giant, slow-moving Galápagos tortoises reminiscent of Volkswagens as they crawled along the dirt trails as if in rush hour traffic; myopic and raucous blue-footed boobies laying eggs the size of tennis balls that we avoided crushing as we stepped cautiously over rocky terrain to overcrowded sea lion colonies; flamingo-carpeted lakes with so many of the birds gathered on their stilt legs that the water surface shimmered with their lipstick-pink hue.

Exhausted, on a beach that was an extra-long-distance swim to reach without ending up as an entrée, I took a nap. The sand was stark white and fine. It was quiet. I was alone. Our sailboat swayed far away in the bay. I had finally escaped the continuous haranguing that bounced around the boat cabin at Sally Ann from Freddy's vitriolic mouth.

To my surprise, he had begun ridiculing her as soon as the journey commenced. In the mornings while I made coffee, he'd start with derogatory comments about her appearance. "You're going to get fat eating so many candy bars," or, "That's a trashy outfit." Or, "You'd look better with a different haircut." *What are you, a fashion consultant?* I'd think. Sally Ann ignored him, which irritated Freddy even more.

I spread out on the hot sand, shedding not only my

swimsuit but the stress of being stuck on that small boat with a contentious couple, and dozed off as the heat and sun melted me into the silky sand. A tapping on my foot woke me—a finch hopped between my feet. Meanwhile, I was being closely observed by a towering blue heron who blocked the sun as he stared down his beak at my supine body. I had also been joined by a fellow sun worshipper: a giant marine iguana lounged next to me, his leathery eyes closed.

As I lay there, feeling hemmed in and claustrophobic, a minute wiggling tickled my thigh. The sand was moving. A little head popped out and furious miniature flippers paddled the sand away from a palm-size baby green sea turtle. I had been napping on a nest. I leapt up, startled by the broiling sands underneath my nude derriere. The sand erupted as a brigade of tiny turtles emerged.

A sea turtle lays up to 110 eggs in each nest under the sand. It takes the concerted effort of at least 50 hatchlings to dig their way up and reach the surface. Sea turtles are phototactic, meaning that they are attracted to light. They are guided by the brightest light, which is usually sunlight reflecting on the sea. That is why they scuttled like mad to the surf, even as frigatebirds dove down and plucked them up like snacks.

Shooing the birds away, I cupped the terrorized baby turtles, soft like kid leather, and threw as many of them as I could into the deeper water so that they might have a chance to swim out to sea and come back here to lay eggs themselves someday.

Of the 50 unique and fearless animal species only found in the Galápagos archipelago—much of which were inspiration for Charles Darwin's theory of natural selection—the penguins were the only creatures that had not actively displayed curiosity toward us humans when we visited them in their colony on Isla Fernandina at the beginning of our trip.

They were small, shy, and adorable as the pair huddled together like lovers when the three of us rowed up to their rocky perch.

"They are real lovebirds, just like us!" Sally Ann exclaimed as Freddy rolled his eyes.

Freddy was surprised there were only two. Where had the others gone? Later, back on the boat, my frayed history book revealed that because of the Galápagos Penguin's smaller size, it has many predators. On land, the penguins must keep an eye out for crabs, snakes, owls, and hawks, while in the water they are preyed upon by sharks, fur seals, and sea lions.

Freddy was subdued the rest of that day, sad about the demise of his penguin friends.

As we sailed from one island to the next, Freddy regaled us with stories of his boyhood exploits. He also bullied Sally Ann. The amazing animal discoveries were tainted by the foul residue from his insults that hung in the air.

Having never been exposed to verbal abuse, it took me awhile to recognize it for what it was—not just a Sanka-induced bad mood.

As I pondered why he would treat his new wife with such cruelty, I guessed that Freddy had been inducted into this school of intimidation by his short-fused father, now affectionately known in my head as "Caveman Reinhart."

Freddy never spoke about his mother.

Oddly, he was nothing but nice to me and delighted in my jubilant excitement about his animal kingdom tour.

After two weeks, the oppressive atmosphere was taking its toll on me. It was like being caught in a really bad sitcom where I was invited to laugh and nod and not react to the pain inflicted on Sally Ann.

One day toward the end of our adventure, I was looking at the horizon, squinting at the bright noonday sun, when I found a squished Manicho in my pack. Leaning against the shady side of the mast, my spine pressed hard and upright against the wood, crunching on the chocolate-covered stale peanuts, I wondered how much more abuse I could witness. "Stupid, don't get your greasy lotion on the deck," Freddy belittled Sally Ann yet again with a sneer. The bombastic tone made me nauseous. I peered around the mast. She was looking down at her perfectly manicured pink toenails. Freddy was pushing his face into hers, trying to get her to look at him, his hands flexed in fists. His neck muscles bulged with a sinewy, aggressive redness.

My eyes narrowed. It was time to end this traveling mess of a honeymoon. I stood up and walked toward him. I raised my hands in slow motion in a trance of fed-up-ness and shoved him hard in the chest, not caring if there were sharks circling. Not caring how or if we would get back to port. He slammed backward off the gunwale into the swirling, chilly, dark-blue waters of the Humboldt Current.

Sally Ann pressed her hand over her mouth and stared at me in shock. "Why did you do that?" she cried.

I did it for me. She didn't want a protector or a savior. She had the dope flailing in the water, whom she was already helping back into the boat.

"Freddy, Freddy, Freddy! Are you all riiiiight?" She crooned it like a Country Western song, holding her hands to her heart and casting a scalding look in my direction.

Sally Ann pulled him into the boat, kissing and caressing him as he emerged from the sea like Neptune. Freddy shook water droplets from his charcoal-black curly hair and looked mystified, as if it didn't register that a 120-pound woman had pushed him, a star college quarterback, overboard.

They were lovebirds, just like those two isolated penguins, the entire two-day sail back to Puerto Ayora. I did not get keelhauled or forced to walk the plank, though I did feel invisible. Freddy never raised his voice to Sally Ann again and she got all doe-eyed and giggly in his presence.

As we pulled up to port, I hugged Sally Ann goodbye. Behind her beauty queen smile rippled embarrassment, humiliation, and warmth mixed with hostility. Freddy was nowhere to be seen, so I quickly threw my bag onto the planks and headed to the store for a beer and a Manicho.

Leaning against a guano-splattered post, I slugged back the lukewarm beer. It had been a hell of a trip. I had witnessed the wild wonders of the Galápagos *and* the wild unpredictable terrain of the heart up close and personal. Freddy Schmidt, with his swagger and drilling voice, was a fine example of Darwin's theory: The biggest, the loudest, the strongest with the most dominating genes wins the fairest maiden.

No wonder I have always been attracted to gay men.

# TWO-STEPPIN' & PUSSY POPPIN'

New Orleans 1977-1982

*Get up*
*Get up*
*Get up*

*Get on up*
*Stay on the scene*

*Get on up*
*Like a sex machine*

It was a rockin' night in the Big Easy. James Brown was belting out his classic funky song as sweat streamed down his animated face. His backup singers were howling, clapping, and shimmying. The horn section pointed to heaven, blowing and smoking as they fogged up the windows of the Delta Queen, a nineteenth-century paddlewheel steamboat. A tarnished copper moon cast rippling light across the water as we churned down the muddy Mississippi River. The frenzied crowd pressed right up to the stage like a rising tide.

And there I was, dancing and singing on top of the throbbing speakers on either side of the stage—best view in the house—making up my own lyrics because James was stuck on repeat. He must have chanted that same stanza a hundred times. Over and over.

*Get up*

*Get up*

*Get up*

*Get on up*

*Get up...*

This was punctuated with an occasional, "Like a sex machine!" or "Shake your money maker!"

Somewhere around the fiftieth repeat was when I started switching it up, singing with an unselfconscious *joie de vivre* that can only come from being well-lubricated on Tanqueray and tonic.

Until someone tugged on my ankle. Opening my eyes and coming out of my funky town trance, I looked down to see a black woman, who had hold of my leg and was shaking it to get my attention. "Shut up, honky!" she shouted, looking like she was going to bite. The sea of faces surrounding her also glared up at me. Was I being sacrilegious or off-key? I supposed either one was a possibility.

I knew I could shake my booty with the best of 'em, so that couldn't be why I'd stirred up a mob scene.

Must be my improvised lyrics:

"Get down."

"Don't get down!"

"Get funky, get real funky. "

"Oh heck, don't get funky."

"Get down."

"Get up."

"For god's sake, I said get down!"

Chirping like a canary, wailing like an opera singer. Keeping time with the man sporting the meringued pompadour—just whimsically altering the lyrics a tad.

Plus, I was busting a new move that a jiving group of twelve-year-old girls in cornrows taught me at the Jazz Fest. I asked them if this snake-like gyration had a name. It was a little disturbing to hear the young girls say, "Pussy Pop" without missing a beat. This sinuous dance step requires a very flexible spine and pelvis. Perfect for the King of Soul's anthem.

The sea of fans below me—all black except for me—did not seem to appreciate my vocal stylings or my *au courant* choreography. Fortunately, I was way off to the side of the stage and James hadn't noticed me...yet.

Okay, I was being passive-aggressive. James and I had a bit of history between us.

Now I felt a finger jabbing my other ankle not being prodded by an infuriated JB fan. I glanced down to see Lloyd Cottingim's bemused face trying to look annoyed with me, and failing miserably. Still, he scowled like an angry pirate and mouthed, "Get down!"

It was all Lloyd's fault that I was up here on these speakers, anyway. Well, not on the speakers. That had been my idea. My inner go-go girl was getting her mojo on. I'd just spent an eternity in the crowded, wire-laid backstage and was sick and tired of hearing the hot music licks without being able to dance.

The reason I was even backstage at all came back to meeting Lloyd, who convinced me to volunteer at the New Orleans Jazz and Heritage Festival. I was charged with picking the performing artists up at the airport, taking them to their hotel, and then their gigs. The vehicle I was given to transport these mostly iconic performers was Lloyd's old but reliable red Chevy pickup truck. Not a limo. We were on a budget.

I had met Lloyd one night several years earlier in 1977, when I went out dancing by myself in San Francisco, where I lived. Clifton Chenier, a Creole French-speaking native of Opelousas, Louisiana, was playing at the Last Day Saloon on Clement Street.

I'd become infatuated with Zydeco music and Cajun dancing when a friend invited me to a black Baptist church. Not knowing what to expect, I walked into a whitewashed clapboard church packed with all ages and types of folks. On the stage was a projection screen, and we took a seat on the hard wooden pews in front of it. A man stood up and introduced himself. It was Les Blank, an ethnographic filmmaker from Berkeley. He was showing his documentary *Hot Peppers*, featuring a musical portrait of Zydeco king Clifton Chenier, and from the first scene I was hooked.

After the film, we pushed the benches away. Les and his friends ladled out red beans and rice in the back of the church while we danced to Clifton, who had driven out from the Big Easy for the occasion. I climbed feet-first onto the Zydeco bandwagon, dancing to Queen Ida, Buckwheat Zydeco, and Clifton whenever they came to the Bay Area and played at small venues like Ashkenaz in Berkeley, and at churches and community halls.

Now, at the Last Day Saloon, I stood in the dark and mostly empty club while Clifton wailed on his *frottoir*—a washboard made of corrugated metal and worn like a vest. He furiously scratched the tin surface with spoons, cranking out Zydeco music. Tapping my foot for only so long, I got out on the dance floor solo. Several lively numbers later, I was joined by a short man with a devilish grin. He offered me his hand and away we went. He could Cajun two-step like a house on fire.

During the break, we propped our sweaty selves against the wooden bar and he treated me to my first Tanqueray and tonic. It was thirst quenching in a cold, limey, quinine kind of way.

In a thick Cajun accent reminiscent of warm maple syrup and butter pooling on slabs of cinnamon French toast, my dance partner introduced himself. "My name is Lloyd Cottingim. I'm from New Orleans. What brings you out to swing to Clifton by yourself?"

Taking a gulp of the tall, refreshing drink, I wiped the beads of sweat from my face and said, "This is dancing music and I'm a dancing fiend. Most of my West Coast friends don't groove to Zydeco."

Lloyd was a ship's engineer and had traveled to San Francisco from the Gulf via the Panama Canal. He told me he usually made it to San Francisco twice a year, and that he went to clubs, looking for live music, wherever he docked.

We danced till Clifton Chenier and his Red Hot Louisiana Band packed up their instruments and drove away in their beater van to the next gig destination. Standing on the sidewalk, still tapping our toes to a silent beat, Lloyd asked, "You want to eat ribs at the ocean? I have some leftovers in the car."

I wasn't attracted to Lloyd. He was troll-like with a scraggly beard, dressed in a faded plaid shirt, baggy jeans, and laced-up lumberjack boots. But I appreciated his Southern drawl, his gentlemanly ways, and his big heart. That night had shown me he was an outstanding dance partner with stamina to match mine. Plus, there was a mischievous spark in his eye, and he liked to have a good time. This turned out to be true for all the Cajuns I met, but he was my first so I didn't yet know how spunky and fun those swamp boys can be.

"Sure. I'm game—and hungry."

We hopped in his rental car and drove to Ocean Beach. Parked facing the crashing waves, we sucked on succulent, sticky ribs from Leon's Barbeque and listened to Keith Jarrett's jazz piano riffs on the tape deck.

By the time the sun rose, a pile of greasy napkins littered the back seat and we had embarked on a friendship that would last more than two decades. We shared a love of music, dancing, food, and conversation—and staying up till the wee dawn hours doing all of the above.

That same morning, over Dungeness crab benedicts and foamy lattés at Mama's in North Beach, Lloyd said, "You gotta come to Jazz Fest. I've worked for the Fest every year since it started in 1970. In fact, Clifton Chenier was part of our first lineup. So were Mahalia Jackson, Duke Ellington, and the Eureka Brass Band."

Lloyd looked at me expectantly, and I nonchalantly sipped my latté. I wasn't sold yet. He tried again, leaning in excitedly, as the café buzzed with early-morning diners.

"My job has gotten pretty hectic since the festival is growing exponentially each year. Three hundred and fifty folks attended the first one when it was held in Beauregard Square, and this year we expect over ninety thousand." He leaned back again, impressed by his own numbers. "It's gotten so big, it's now held at the Fair Grounds Race Course—a hundred-and-forty-five--acre site. Yeah, baby!"

"So what do you need me for?" I asked, a little suspiciously.

Lloyd folded his arms. "I could use an assistant. You can help chauffeur the performers around New Orleans and stay at my house. It's the end of April and goes for two weekends, but you should come for a month and I'll show you around Louisiana. It's like a foreign country."

I counted the weeks until April in my head—eight—secure in the knowledge that I could leave my retail stores in the trusted hands of my employees, and took a long, assessing look at Lloyd. Could I trust that he did not have an ulterior motive? I asked, "You serious? Even if it is platonic with no hope of me ending up in your bed?"

He chuckled and said, "No problem. I have lots of girlfriends. My bedroom skills make me popular with the ladies."

"Too much information," I said, rolling my eyes.

He added, a smile twitching at the corners of his

mouth, "I'm fine with just being friends. You'll dig New Orleans and the Jazz Fest. It's Mecca for music hounds."

Lloyd would be true to his word and never tried to jump my bones. But I didn't know this about him yet. I just had to trust his generous and tempting offer. He'd already lured me with his fancy footwork and the late-night rib fest by the beach, and he knew my real weakness: dancing to live, soulful ethnic music until the early hours of the morning.

The next day I bought an airplane ticket.

Two months later, Lloyd picked me up at the New Orleans International Airport. He looked exactly the same as he did when I met him in San Francisco, except that he had traded in the long-sleeve plaid shirt for a wrinkly short-sleeve Hawaiian number in a faded orange hibiscus flower print. He greeted me with a huge bear hug that lifted me off the ground, even though I was taller than him. His red truck idled at the curb.

First stop was Buster Holmes' restaurant in the French Quarter for red beans and rice with smoked sausage and turnip greens. Afterward we strolled down to Angelo Brocato's on Ursulines Street for cannolis and lemon ice. My initiation into all things New Orleans had begun. We then drove over to the Thirteenth Ward, where he had grown up near the Neville Brothers.

After pointing out the rickety double-shotgun-style house he was raised in and waving to a few old acquaintances hanging out on their front porches, sipping Barq's root beer from bottles, we cruised over to St. Charles Avenue.

"You don't mind if I do some work?" he said as we

drove.

"Are we going to one of the ships you work on?"

Tossing the toothpick he had been cleaning his teeth with out the window, he said, "No. I'm also a city building inspector. I check out the historic houses that are getting a facelift and write up reports."

I was trying to figure out how he juggled so many diverse jobs at the same time when we pulled up to an ornate, tilted Queen Anne on the edge of the Garden District.

Lloyd got out and walked around to my side of the truck. The door was stuck shut, but it sprang open when he gave it a hard, noisy kick with the same lumberjack boot he was wearing when I met him on the dance floor in San Francisco. We sauntered up the crooked wooden steps and he knocked.

Heavy, shuffling footsteps and a high-pitched voice trilled, "Don't let the cat out!" The door creaked open. A statuesque, barefoot man in a black silk kimono embroidered with chrysanthemums greeted us, just as a fat tabby ran between his legs and escaped onto the street.

"Lloyd! My *favorite* city employee! Are you here to check my pipes?"

Lloyd blushed. "Armand, you are such a tease! Meet my California assistant. She flew all the way here from San Francisco to help me at the Fest. It's her first one."

Clapping his hand to his forehead, Armand said, "Oh my, a Fest virgin. Be prepared for one crazy time if Lloyd is in charge of your itinerary. You won't be a virgin for long!"

As Armand leaned forward to grasp my hand, his

kimono fell open, revealing a hairy chest, six-pack abs, and a g-string.

"Where's my belt?" Armand fussed as he waved us inside.

"Would you like chicory coffee with a dollop of Baileys Irish Cream, or gin martinis?"

Though it was early afternoon, the drawing room was dark with its heavy, red velvet curtains drawn and crystal chandeliers shedding dim light. Large gilt mirrors reflected our shadowy, distorted images. I felt small and ordinary compared to our host, who was still clucking and chuckling about me being a "virgin." Lloyd went to check the kitchen remodel and I sat across from Armand on a leopard-print divan. He had still not belted his robe shut as he poured martinis into three bathtub-size glasses.

We toasted to my first Fest and then Armand gushed, "Tell me all about Frisco! In the 1960s I performed there at Finocchio's on Broadway in a drag queen revue."

Two hours later, we stumbled outside into the stark sunlight. I squinted at Lloyd and asked, "Are all the homeowners of the houses you inspect such hospitable characters?"

As he giddily skipped down the steps a bit lopsided, he said, "I pass every building permit application. I know everybody in this town. How can I not help them out? I get a lot of perks, too. From coffee cake to cash; sex to music." He winked and nodded toward Armand's house. "Even martinis!"

We drove to several other houses in the Garden District and Lloyd explained their architectural styles and history. "This was the biggest Confederate city in the

South. Barely a year after the Civil War started, New Orleans was captured without combat or bombardment. As a result, we have the largest collection of surviving Antebellum architecture."

These architectural grand dames kept company with enormous, ancient oak trees that spread protective, leafy arms over charmingly disheveled gardens hedged in rhododendrons, azaleas, and camellias. Dark-leafed magnolia trees in full bloom shed handkerchief-sized ivory petals on the emerald-green lawns. Lloyd pointed to a Victorian painted a lurid lavender and said, "This home was built in 1857 for a wealthy merchant, who shot and killed himself on the front porch after running into financial trouble." He pointed to a throng of people looking up at the house. "That group of tourists milling around on the sidewalk are on a 'haunted house' walking tour."

Just as we slowed to a stop in front of the Victorian, I heard the guide announce to his flock in a tremulous tone, "I have seen a misty form float across the front porch, so keep your eyes unfocused yet focused."

I laughed and said, "I'm surprised the tour is during the day."

We continued on to the funkier Marigny and Bywater neighborhoods on the other side of the French Quarter, stopping at hulky Greek Revivals and narrow shotgun shacks made from swamp cypress during the Civil War era that were on Lloyd's inspection list. Most of the owners or contractors weren't home, so he left chatty, hand-written notes on their door, each signed with his curlicue signature and a happy face. He certainly didn't act like any government official I'd ever met.

Getting back into the truck with a groan after his last stop, where they plied us with hot, sugary beignets, he said, "How about I take you to the Jazz Fest offices and introduce you to the staff? If we're lucky, Gus will be deep-frying his famously tasty turkeys."

Balancing out the martinis and beignets with substantial food sounded like a good idea. It was beginning to occur to me that I would have to throw my regular California diet of fresh, organic salads and whole grains to the wind while here in the Deep South.

The office at the fairgrounds was in chaos. The frantic staff was juggling all the last-minute logistics of running one of the most popular music festivals in the world, with bands flying in from as far away as Senegal, Belize, and Madagascar.

Lloyd pushed open the screen door and said to everybody in the makeshift trailer office, "Meet my volunteer assistant from San Francisco."

Quint Davis, the Fest producer, came over and I felt an immediate attraction. His sleeves were rolled up and he was talking on two phones at once and rolling his eyes, but managed to give me a warm smile. He handed the phones to a staffer and said, "Welcome to the hub of the bedlam! We're all meeting up at the Rock'n'Bowl later tonight. Why don't you join us so we can all get to know you a bit more?" I nodded, grinning. "Good!" he said. "Now, it's back to work."

My palms were sweaty from the encounter with Quint and the humidity. I turned away and followed Lloyd over to his desk. He picked up the roster of the musicians we'd be shuttling between the airport, their lodgings, and performance venues, and I looked over his shoulder and whistled. It was a veritable *Who's Who* in the music world: Dr. John, Duke Ellington, Youssou N'Dour, Branford Marsalis, Linda Ronstadt, Miles Davis, Aretha Franklin, Tito Puente, The Temptations, Ella Fitzgerald. "Who *isn't* on this list?" I said. Lloyd raised his eyebrows, his grin practically saying, "I told you so."

A tantalizing, meaty aroma emanated from the parking lot. Distracted, Lloyd handed me the clipboard and went outside where a hefty man wearing overalls, with a sweaty red face, auburn hair, sideburns, and a beard, was prodding a rotund turkey that bobbed in a boiling vat of fat with a long, metal fork. The fryer was a custom-made behemoth that looked like a locomotive belching savory-smelling smoke.

"Hey Lloyd, what's up?" the man said and slapped Lloyd hard on the back.

"Easy, Gus, I don't want to fall in the fryer." They both guffawed in that wheezy geezer-guy way, like what he said was the funniest thing they'd both ever heard. Lloyd nodded to the bird. "Got any turkey ready to eat for me and my friend?"

"Yeah, go on inside my trailer. There's a hot platter piled high. Help yourself. Cold Jax beer is in the fridge."

The trailer was dark. I tripped over two German Shepherds huddled together, gnawing on turkey legs. They gave a low growl, scurried under the dining table, and continued demolishing the bones with loud crunching sounds.

We crowded around the Formica table, careful to keep

our feet away from the dogs, and dug in using paper towels for plates. Lloyd grabbed a drumstick and said, "I could devour an entire tom."

"So what's Quint's story?" I asked, trying to sound casual, while Lloyd inhaled his food.

After he swallowed, he cocked his head and raised an eyebrow. "Interested, eh? Don't get your hopes up; I think he's engaged to Linda Ronstadt."

I giggled nervously. "Oh, well. Don't think I'll win that contest."

After he had polished off the platter and two beers, he burped and I asked, "Why does Gus fry the turkey?"

Lloyd leaned back against the banquette and said, "He insists baked turkey is too dry and bland for Cajun tastes. Unlike roast turkey, a quickly cooked deep-fried turkey is rich in flavor, with a crispy, golden-brown skin and tender, juicy interior."

Mouth full of the delectable meat, I could only nod my head in agreement as Lloyd continued, "Gus McIlhenny's family has been making Tabasco Sauce since 1869. He lives on Avery Island and is heir to a huge fortune. But all Gus really wants to do is live in this trailer with his dogs and fry turkeys for his friends. He loves feeding people!"

Licking the salty and spicy grease off my fingers, I exclaimed with a satiated sigh, "That was the best turkey I've ever eaten. What's Gus's marinade?"

"Well, it's a secret. He won't share the recipe with anyone. Even for front-row Rolling Stones tickets...I tried. I suspect it includes a lot of his family's red-hot pepper sauce."

We threw our bones under the table to the voracious

dogs and went outside to thank Gus, who was busy trussing another turkey for the fryer.

"See you at the Rock'n'Bowl," Lloyd yelled through the office screen door.

We headed back Uptown to take a nap before going out dancing, making one pit stop to nab a few slices of oozing pecan pie topped with whipped cream at the Camellia Grill, down the street from his house on Carrollton Avenue.

As we clumped up the rickety staircase to his front door, an elderly woman in a faded flower-print nightgown leaned out of a second-story window across the alley. An ashy cigarette dangled from the side of her mouth.

Lloyd waved. "How you doing today, Miss Ermaline?"

Bleary-eyed, she hacked and said, "Peachy, Lloyd. Thanks for askin'."

She stared at me, shaking her head. "Who's the new girlie you got there? And why is she following you around with a clipboard and a suitcase?"

"She's my assistant."

Ermaline humphed and said, "Right... and I'm your chauffeur." With a sly cackle, she added, "Got any pot?"

Once he reached the top of the steps, Lloyd rummaged around in his briefcase and yelled, "Catch." He tossed Ermaline a baggie, which she snapped out of the air like a gator swallowing a leaping frog.

"Thanks, Lloyd. You can deduct it from my next paycheck." She giggled girlishly, then disappeared inside and shut the window with a thud.

"Well, I won't be seeing that money any time soon,"

Lloyd grouched.

Why did I get the feeling this was another of Lloyd's "jobs"?

Ermaline wasn't the only one who loved her marijuana. After Lloyd got me set up in the guest bedroom, he went into the living room. He sat in his great-grandfather's rocking chair, placed an upside-down shoebox lid on his lap, and neatly rolled several thin joints, all the while rocking back and forth. The inch-deep grooves in the hardwood floor were evidence that this was where he had spent several decades rocking and rolling, smoking and reading. I discovered that Lloyd was a night owl and barely slept; hence he was one of the most well-read people I'd ever met. He was filled with facts and details on a myriad of topics—a human encyclopedia. It was one of the reasons he was such a good conversationalist.

That night, we sauntered down the street to the Rock'n'Bowl in the warm evening air faintly scented with river detritus and night-blooming jasmine. Even though I was tuckered out from our gallivanting around town and didn't really want to bump into the possibly engaged Quint, Lloyd insisted that I hear Professor Longhair—yet another New Orleans legend.

"How could a music club be in a bowling alley?" I asked. "Won't the crashing pins and bouncing bowling balls drown out the music?"

Lloyd shook his head and hooked his finger, motioning me to follow him inside the noisy club. Downstairs was well-lit, with several groups of people queuing around the lanes. Upstairs was dark. There was a stage and a dance floor with chrome tables scattered about.

It was around midnight, and an elderly man sat on a piano bench muttering to the audience. He wore sunglasses and was hunched over the upright piano. He began to play and the place lit up. This skinny old man with the gold-toothed smile rocked the house with his Mardi Gras second-linin' music—his fingers rolling, hopping, and pecking over the keys like jumping beans. We pushed the tables aside and cut loose. Along with Lloyd, there was a plethora of great dance partners who kept me two-stepping to every hot number.

Our dance-a-thon was interrupted when Professor Longhair suddenly stopped playing. We all turned around in mid-step and saw that a woman had gotten on stage. We heard her ask if she could sing with him, and he nodded and began tinkling the keys. The woman joined in. It was the unmistakable voice of Rickie Lee Jones.

None of the Jazz Fest staff ended up coming that night, but who needed them? Any thought of Quint Davis was danced out of my mind, accompanied by the sweet musical coupling of Longhair and Jones.

These impromptu jam sessions happened night after night at every club we went to. Lloyd was right: New Orleans was the mother lode for live music. Add to the mix all the stellar musicians performing at the Jazz Fest, who then spontaneously dropped into the clubs for a spot of improv, and it was pure overload.

My job started the day after my first experience at the Rock'n'Bowl with a run to the airport to pick up Flora Purim, the Brazilian jazz singer. I already had her solo album and was nervous to meet one of my main divas. She was unmistakable as she glided into the arrival lounge in a long, white cotton dress, her many bracelets jangling. I introduced myself and she sashayed after me toward the red truck. For once in its creaky, rusty existence, the door opened effortlessly. She lifted her flowing skirt and lithely hopped onto the bench seat. I was worried she might be put off by our outdated wheels but she rolled down the window, turned to me with a broad, sunlit smile and said, "I love Louisiana already!"

She chatted about her life on the drive into town, and white cranes flew over the truck when we drove along the Lake Pontchartrain Causeway. "Oh, such a good omen!" she exclaimed delightedly. The briny smell of shrimp and brackish water floated in through the open windows.

Her soft, lilting accent soothed my discomfort with being so close to one of my favorite singers. "Are you hungry?" I asked. Her performance wasn't until that night. She nodded.

We drove straight to Buster's, where Lloyd had introduced me to red beans and rice just the day before. It only cost a dollar a plate, but they were the tastiest beans in the South. Flora said, "This dish reminds me of *feijoada*—Brazilian bean stew." Sweat beaded on the icy beer bottles as we feasted and yakked about our travels.

Flora and I hit it off. I had hitchhiked through Brazil in the early 1970s and spent two weeks dancing in the streets of Salvador da Bahia during Carnival. We had a lot to talk about.

We drove to the hotel and later I picked Flora up and took her to her performance. She extended her trip three extra days and asked if I would show her around town. I told her we could discover New Orleans together with Lloyd's guidance. After nights of clubbing, during which Flora got on stage to warble with Irma Thomas; Dr. John; and Rockin' Dopsie, Jr. & The Zydeco Twisters, we'd eat greasy pre-dawn breakfasts at the Hummingbird Grill, a twenty-four-hour diner in Skid Row where sleepless heroin addicts sniffled over their coffee. I dropped Flora off at the airport and she invited me to her and her husband Airto Moreira's show in San Francisco a month later.

I was developing a reputation at the Fest office of being an exceptional shepherd to the musicians. Lloyd was very proud of his acolyte. After the festival ended, I flew back to California and my busy life, promising Lloyd I'd come back and work for him again. I kept that promise five years in a row.

On one of my annual visits, I got assigned to escort Cab Calloway around town. It was a big day for me. I'd watched him dance and sing on The Ed Sullivan Show in 1967, performing "Minnie the Moocher." Looking slick in a white tuxedo, he'd scat-sing while doing a gliding backstep—the precursor to Michael Jackson's "moonwalk."

He was shorter and greyer than I remembered when I met Cab at the airport, but still debonair decked out in his trademark tuxedo.

He didn't blink when I ushered him out to the red truck. He graciously opened my door, then went around to his side. Miraculously, the door cooperated without the usual persuasive kick. Cab lifted his tails and swept onto the seat.

As with Flora, I developed an immediate friendship with Cab. We'd sit in the cool, dark recesses of his hotel lounge, sipping cocktails, and he'd regale me with insider stories of the jazz world from the 1930s when he played in Duke Ellington's band and headlined at the Cotton Club— New York's premier jazz scene. As I nibbled on a syrupy maraschino cherry, Cab's seductive, smoky voice wove a cocoon around me, revealing another era of cigarette holders and furs, big bands and Bing Crosby. Then we'd go to the Maple Leaf and eat a dozen raw oysters at the bar for ten cents apiece while listening to Aaron Neville croon "Tell It Like It Is."

Before I drove him back to his hotel, we'd stroll under the moonlight, looking beyond the levee at the silvery fish-scale whitecaps flitting across the Mississippi. The river was six feet higher than the street, and the only thing between us and being under water was a packed-down pile of dirt. Cab and I would shake our heads and marvel at the feat of engineering keeping all that water at bay.

On my very last trip to the Jazz Fest in 1982, I found the atmosphere of New Orleans had changed.

That year Laura, Lloyd's new wife and the head of operations for the Jazz Fest, picked me up at the airport. Lloyd was busy chauffeuring Dizzy Gillespie around town.

I'd be staying at their new home in Algiers Point—a free ferry ride across the river from the French Quarter.

Before I even settled myself in the front seat of the faithful ole red truck she said, "Promise me you will not walk by yourself everywhere at all hours like you usually do. This town has gotten really dangerous."

At a stoplight on Decatur Street, Laura reached into her purse and showed me her handgun.

I raised my eyebrows. "Since when did you start carrying a gun?"

"Since crack cocaine showed up on the street," she replied matter-of-factly.

Just then, a hulking man in a shiny tracksuit threw himself across the hood of the car. Gripping the wipers, he pressed his acne-scarred face against the windshield. Several teeth were missing. Wild-eyed he screamed, "Bitches!"

"See what I mean?" Laura said calmly as she tromped on the accelerator.

The crazed man bounced off the hood like a ping-pong ball and rolled back into the gutter.

Laura didn't break a sweat—or glance in the rearview mirror.

She said sternly, "You will not go out at night by yourself! Capiche?"

I did go out that night with Lloyd and Laura for a seasonal treat of soft-shell crab meuniére at Mandina's, and then on to Tipitina's to dance ourselves sweaty-silly to the drunk and opiate-laced powerhouse Etta James. Her bawdy lyrics made me blush.

The next morning, Lloyd shook me awake. He waved croissants and black coffee under my nose as I rose from the creaky couch. "Get up, lazy. James Brown is arriving at the airport in one hour and you're picking him up."

I got there just as the plane landed. I waited and waited. Everyone had debarked and departed. The only person left in the deserted lounge was a short, older woman wearing a maroon pantsuit with sturdy pumps and a handbag. Swiveling her head in all directions, she turned and made eye contact with me. She had a creased, mahogany face framed by a bouffant hairdo, and looked vaguely familiar.

Then it struck me. That was the same face on the cover of James Brown's *Sex Machine*. An album I played incessantly when I was a teenager in 1970.

It must be his mother or... "Mr. Brown?" I hesitantly queried as he turned again and stared at me in disbelief.

"Where's my driver?" he screeched without bothering to say hello or ask my name. He looked poised to hit me with his shiny patent leather handbag.

Trying to keep the welcoming smile from sliding off my face, I politely said, "Sorry, I didn't recognize you from the back, but I do work for Jazz Fest. I'll be taking you to the hotel."

This did not soften his dour expression. Taking a deep breath, I turned and walked outside to the curb. Though boiling mad, he followed me to the truck, and I opened the door with only one well-aimed kick.

He looked horrified and squawked, "You're just a girl! You can't be my driver, and this jalopy can't be my ride. Where's my limo?"

Somehow, I herded him into the truck. I tried to strike up a conversation but he didn't say another word on the drive into New Orleans, although he made a lot of huffy noises and kept patting his stiff hair back into place. The windows were wide open, as the air conditioning didn't work. With great relief, I dropped him off at his hotel.

Later, I heard from the Fest management and stage crews that he was indeed a demanding pain-in-the-ass. He also made a point of telling them he did not want to be chauffeured around by "that girl in the truck."

I didn't have the pleasure of encountering Mr. Brown again until my night dancing on those speakers, cruising down the moonlit Mississippi.

Temperamental pain-in-the-ass he might be, but I had to appreciate his showmanship and ability to work the crowd into a froth of moaning, gyrating, screaming, and Pussy Poppin'.

*Get on up*
*Get up*
*Shake your arm*
*Then use your form*
*Stay on the scene like a sex machine.*

As he *finally* ended the song and the sex machine ground to a halt, I sheepishly slid off the speakers and slunk backstage out of sight, Lloyd shaking his head after me. After all, that crowd was there to see the King of Soul, not the honky from California. He may have been a huffy, cantankerous grandma with me, but for them, he was the original sex machine.

# TWO MUHAMMADS

Morocco 1983

"I want son just like this!" *Thump, thump, thump.*

Galen's chest resounded like a Taiko drum as the turbaned and mustachioed man in a floor-length pale-blue robe pounded my son's back with the flat of his creased palm. He raised him high in the air, showing the other men in the tent our eight-month-old baby. The Berber tribal leader proclaimed what sounded like, *"Willy Muhammad! Willy Muhammad!"* He'd yell this out periodically as he pumped Galen up and down in his arms. Stubby baby legs dangling and tiny hands flapping, Galen chortled, probably associating the movements with the flying airplane game where we'd lift him over our heads and dip and swoop him around the room.

Usually he was reluctant to let strangers hold him—especially loud and hairy folk—but for some reason the tall, turbaned chieftain with a firm grip on his torso didn't scare Galen. His big blue eyes gazed steadily at the throng of men congratulating him on his magnificent, though still infant-sized, rib cage and chest.

More thumping and then they escorted Andy, my husband, and me out of the tent and closed the flaps behind us, still holding Galen on high like a flag of baby boy perfection. Chanting emanated from within the massive slate-black tent. I stood on high alert outside the sealed tent flap, waiting to spring forward if I heard a cry or a whimper. When I peeked into the lantern-lit interior, he was sitting on a Berber rug in the center of a ring formed by the dark-eyed men, who were drumming on taut goatskin tars. Galen seemed to be enjoying his princely role and the adoring circle of clansmen swaying in a rhythmic trance around him. A smile graced his face as he watched them with utter equanimity.

I let go of the flap and released a sigh. How did this blond baby Buddha end up being serenaded in a Berber tent high in the Atlas Mountains?

Both my husband and I were seasoned travelers and professional travel writers, and we often ported Galen nonchalantly to remote corners of the globe. We'd pack his toys and diapers, carriers and strollers, and trundle him onto the airplane, this time heading to Morocco on a Royal Air Maroc flight from New York to Marrakech.

Galen was easy to travel with, as he hadn't started walking yet. He lay in my lap, noisily nursing the entire eight-hour flight. It was the bearded guy sitting next to me who was problematic. Oblivious to the fact that his rough and gamey-smelling wool robe was billowing over both of our seats, smothering me and my baby, he constantly rocked back and forth in his seat, muttering his prayers. He was not the only devout man on the plane. It was hard to reach the bathroom, clogged as the aisles were with prostrate Muslims accordioned onto tiny prayer rugs. I'd gather up Galen, and my courage, and get ready for the gauntlet, my internal voice muttering, "Excuse me while I leap over you and—oops—kick off your turban. I know, I, a mere female, shouldn't touch you or look you in the eyes, but it's a challenge to pretend you aren't blocking the aisle when I have to change my baby's diaper." Many had calloused bumps on their foreheads from pressing their faces onto the prayer rug five times a day while facing Mecca—which, in an airplane, must have been a challenge. I was told it is an emblem of pride to have these grotesque grayish growths protruding above their eyes. The guy sitting next to me won the piety award, as he had the most pronounced lump of any of the prostrates. It was the size of a doughnut, ringed with cracked, yellowing, glue-like edges.

A travel writer friend had piqued our interest one late night around the fire, wine flowing freely, with the story of an ancient tribal festival in Morocco that few foreigners had heard about in a region that didn't encourage tourism—being as it was in the middle of nowhere with no hotels or paved roads. We decided this would be the perfect destination for our next off-the-beaten-path-adventure-with-a-baby.

The Imilchil betrothal fair has been held annually for millennia in the heart of the High Atlas Mountains. Every September, neighboring tribes come together in a festival in which women are allowed to "choose" their husbands. The legend behind this tradition is that two young lovers were forbidden to see each other by their warring families. The lovers cried themselves to death, and their tears formed the lakes of Isli ("his") and Tislit ("hers") near Imilchil. Chastened by the young peoples' tragic end, the families dedicated a day every year on the anniversary of the lovers' deaths on which people of different tribes could marry each other of their own free will.

Thousands of Berber tribesmen travel to Imilchil by camel, horse, donkey, and jeep to socialize and pair up their children—a tribal "Dating Game" with dowries. Who wants to go to Disneyland when you can walk among woven camel hair tents with thousands of Berbers smoking hookahs and shouting, trading and cooking, and, just for the fun of it, firing antique muskets into the sky— their celebratory equivalent of fireworks. And when you are hungry, exceptionally fragrant and hearty lamb tajines simmering in aromatic mountain herbs beckon you toward the cook fires.

Several days after our annoying and uncomfortable flight, we rented a car and drove ten hours north to Fez— the gateway city to the mountains where the festival is held.

After settling into a hotel, and with Galen and his road-weary father asleep, I wandered down to the quiet, softly lit bar to decompress. As I sipped a glass of Clariet de Meknès, a delicate pink-hued wine mimicking the light French style, a dashing man in a khaki safari outfit came over and introduced himself.

With a slight bow, he said, *"Bonsoir*, my name is Driss.

Are you Norwegian?"

"Why no—American—but I do have a healthy dose of Norwegian Viking in my bloodline."

Driss nodded and said, "Ah, that explains the high, sculpted cheekbones."

I wondered if this was a sophisticated pick-up line— yet his polite demeanor and gentle smile did not suggest lechery.

I asked what he was doing in Fez. "I live in Paris but was born in Morocco," he explained. "I'm going to visit my father up in the Atlas."

Startled, I said, "That's where I am going."

His eyes widened, sending his bushy black eyebrows up to his scalp line. "Why?"

I tried not to smile. He made it sound like I had announced I was going to Pumpkin Center, California. "The Imilchil betrothal fair."

"Really? That is exactly where I'm going." He took a swig from his club soda as he sat down next to me and asked, "Do you have a driver and a jeep?"

"No, just a rattletrap hoopty rental car from Marrakech and an international driver's license."

Driss shook his head with a doubtful expression. "Are you familiar with the route?"

"No, but I have a map."

"You won't make it there. It is very dangerous. The wadis have flash floods, the streambeds are already full, and it is freezing at night."

As I sipped the shell-pink drink, I reflected on this dire news.

He filled in the silence by asking, "Do you have

camping gear?"

"No."

His cheeks puffed out and a buffalo-like huff escaped his tightly pursed lips. His brows bunched up like storm clouds gathering on his smooth forehead.

I didn't add that I was with my family and that we did have a vast array of baby accoutrements—enough to open a Toys R Us.

Chivalrously he stood up, thumped his fist on the bar top, making my wine glass jump, and announced with an affirmative nod, "I will take you there."

Though touched and genuinely interested in his offer, I felt the need to back up a bit. "Thank you," I said, trying not to make a commitment with the words. I gestured in a friendly fashion with my free hand, taking a sip of wine with the other. "Tell me more about your family and how you ended up living in Paris."

Nodding gamely, Driss ordered another round.

Though educated in England and currently living in France Driss, a serious and studious chap who became a geologist, was born deep in the Atlas in a cave while his father's tribe fought the French to gain independence in the 1950s. He told me of growing up with real rifles and daggers for toys. That was his idea of childhood—a far cry from Galen's reality of being raised in an American suburb, I thought.

My mind was made up. He would be the perfect guide for us. Still, I couldn't help but grin at the serendipity that had arisen from my need for a soothing glass of good wine.

It was 1983 and I was a San Franciscan. I grew up

baking whole-grain bread, dancing in Golden Gate Park at Be-Ins, and running through redwood groves naked. Plastic diapers and Gerber baby food were not part of my reality. I didn't believe in plastic anything or processed food, so I nursed Galen and on our trips, we carried the soiled cotton diapers with us and washed them at the hotels. The maids hated us.

On the other hand there was Driss, who was thirty years old, handsome, and spoke fluent English, French, Italian, Arabic, as well as Tamazight, his native language. This man was brainy, but he was about to get an education of a whole other sort. I felt a slight stab of guilt that he had no idea what he was getting himself into.

As the conversation dwindled, I thought I should make a perfunctory disclosure as to the scope of our traveling circus, and also clarify that I was not single, in case that was a clincher for him. "I'm with my family. They're asleep in the room. Do you have space in your car for all three of us?"

His expression didn't change, but he said firmly, "Yes, yes. My Land Rover is spacious and I have extra camping gear." It didn't appear to matter to him who these two other people were. He looked at his watch, then got up from his stool. "Rendezvous with me in the lobby at seven a.m. tomorrow," he said, paying our tab. "And eat a hearty breakfast."

The next morning, Andy looked at me skeptically through still-half-closed eyelids when I threw open the drapes and announced, "We have a ride to Imilchil in a jeep with a real Berber. I met him in the bar last night."

"What?"

"He said we can't drive that worthless jalopy we rented into the mountains. The roads are unpaved, there are flashfloods, and we need camping gear. Luckily, he will take us. He's going there to meet his tribe."

Andy just stared at me.

"Quick, get dressed. We have to eat breakfast and then meet him in one hour."

I bundled our rosy-cheeked, sleep-kissed son in a 100% organic, non-dyed cotton blanket and nursed him while drinking mud-black espresso in multiple snail-size demitasses.

When Driss joined us in the lobby, he looked astonished to see an infant and a husband and a mountain of poorly packed stuff. Not only had I not explained our exact family logistics last night, neither had I described our penchant to throw things helter-skelter into overstuffed, oversized duffel bags.

After readjusting his bewildered expression, he reached out his hand to shake Andy's in a firm, reassuring grip that seemed to ease Andy's skepticism that I had actually rounded us up a legitimate ride. He had been reluctant to just toss our possessions into another vehicle and spend the next four days traveling to a remote mountainous region of Morocco with a stranger.

After we crammed ourselves into his highly polished Land Rover and started driving toward the silhouette of the elephantine mountain range looming to the east, I discreetly stuck Galen's head under my blouse. I caught Driss' eyes—just once—looking at us before glancing hurriedly away, his Groucho Marx eyebrows knitted in horror and confusion at the sight of an American woman breastfeeding her son in his back seat.

Andy sat in the front, his tension dissolving as we drove out of town in a vehicle much more comfortable, and safer, than the cranky clunker we had left in the hotel parking lot. He and Driss talked avidly about Sufism, and other religions. It fascinated Driss that Andy was Jewish but practiced Sufism and had traveled throughout the Middle East to study with mystical Sufi scholars. I could tell he was delighted and amused by our whimsical trip to the Atlas with a baby, and that he was genuinely beginning to enjoy our befuddled yet trusting travel style.

Driss enthusiastically pointed out various caverns where his father had hidden while fighting the French. We begged him for details and made him stop the jeep at each place that held a story from his warring, nomadic youth. He guided us along the stony trails where he had herded livestock up to high-altitude mountain pastures, leading him to discover the veins of crystals and fossils that had inspired him to become a geologist.

I dug around in one of our duffel bags and pulled out a super-sized crystal that we had purchased from a pack of goat-herding children on the side of the road between Marrakech and Fez. There was a story behind this crystal, I told Driss. The children had waved us to a stop and run to the car, holding sparkly, deep-purple amethyst crystals that they were selling for a dollar. Andy and I bought the biggest one and drove off feeling like we'd scored a major treasure. I held it in my hands, marveling at its perfect purply crystal interior.

It was hot in the car. The air conditioning wasn't functioning. Sweat beaded on my forehead and my palms got clammy. That's when I noticed my skin was turning purple. Worried that I had contracted a strange disease, I made Andy stop the car and take a look at my hands. After inspecting them carefully, he picked up the crystal sitting in my lap. The amethyst was fading to a pale lavender, and my palms were turning magenta. A stain of purple bloomed across my cotton trousers.

Driss howled with laughter and slapped his thigh, causing Galen to stop nursing when we nearly drove into a ditch. Driss caught his breath and said, "I used to do that trick to tourists, too. But I dyed mine orange to be different. I would tell them it was a rare fire-opal crystal from a rebel's hideaway."

He put our ordinary crystal rock on the dashboard as a talisman and a good joke.

The road was ripped by water troughs, slippery with scree. Large boulders were expertly skirted. We climbed and climbed a staircase-like route—narrow, muddy, rutted. The jeep jolted and jounced through ravines of striated pink and yellow rock.

As Galen dozed, lulled by the rocking ride, Andy and I studied the passing moonscape. Driss broke our reverie by asking, "Why do you travel with your baby and all this luggage to places far away from your home?"

I thought he was being polite calling our smelly diaper sack and other odd assortment of bulging bags "luggage."

Andy didn't answer, so I piped up, "Even though we both grew up in middle-class families in America, I guess we're nomads at heart and are happiest when wandering in foreign cultures. Luckily, our son seems to enjoy it, too."

Driss smiled in the rearview mirror, though he still didn't dare look back at me. "We are very much alike. I love foreign cultures. I hope I will meet a wife who wants to travel with our children—but it will probably not be at Imilchil—so don't get any ideas!"

At dusk, we reached the lip of the rift, known as the "plateau des lacs," at an elevation of 2,119 meters. A scene from *One Thousand and One Nights* throbbed below in the mile-long valley of Assif Melloul ("white river"). Thousand-head herds of horses, camels, and goats milled about, restlessly stomping, their pawing hoofs raising a taupe-tinted veil of dust. Bleating and hawing drifted upward in a cacophony of sounds highlighted by hoots, rifle fire, cymbals, and banging drums. A legion of black tents cut a swath through the center of the valley that was pulsing with revelry.

Galen once again stopped suckling, sensing this phantasmagorical scene pulling us downward onto the alluvial plain. I held him up to look and Galen screeched in delight at the anthem of mayhem arising from the vast valley floor. When we reached the outskirts of the encampment, he bounced up and down holding onto the window edge, excited to see the cartoonish bearded camels flirtatiously blinking their long-lashed orbs. Swaggering Berbers sporting curved daggers gathered around our vehicle, peering in at the foreigners. We slowly drove into the vortex.

There was a rush and doors flew open, and Driss was pulled out of the jeep by brothers and cousins and uncles. Driss introduced us to the flanks of relatives that poured forth to slap his back and raise eyebrows in our direction.

Galen was an immediate rock star, swept up by the tribal leader, who was eager to introduce him to his comrades in the grand meeting tent.

Driss didn't seem fazed that Galen was being carried off with exuberant fanfare, so we weren't either. While he set up camp, he encouraged us to follow Galen's entourage.

As Andy and I waited outside the tent for Galen to be returned to our arms, the temperature plummeted and a silver moon rose from behind the ragged mountain peaks. Driss had understated the weather conditions. It was bone-chilling, with high winds delivering frigid, face-slapping blasts.

Driss insisted that Galen and I sleep in the inner tent sanctum on his bedroll with most of the blankets and sheepskins he had brought for himself. He and Andy retired to the outer tent, wearing all their clothes to keep warm. They stayed up, pacing around the bonfires, drinking gallons of scalding mint tea. Volleys of rifle fire crackled through the hoarfrost encrusting the starry night air. Sleep eluded all but Galen in his baby oblivion.

The next morning, steaming tin cups of thick, dark coffee warmed our hands. With Galen perched in a pack on Andy's back, we wandered through the maze of tents, everything covered in a fine silt stirred up by the snorting horses that galloped through camp, their riders whooping and hollering while waving muskets above their heads.

Warrior blood flows through the Berbers' veins. Berber is derived from the Latin word "Barbari," or barbarians—a title given to them almost 2,000 years ago by invading Roman armies, who were repeatedly attacked by a race of fiercely independent tribes. Many Berbers call themselves some variant of the word *imazighen*, meaning "free people" or "free and noble men," and their symbol is that of a man holding his arms to the sky—a free man. A man who will not be conquered.

We were ushered into a low-hanging tent by a group of tittering women bedecked in silver jewelry, their eyes rimmed in kohl, and geometric, smoky-blue tattoos on their face, hands, and feet. Driss had told us that some Berber tribes tattoo the women's chins to indicate whether she is married or divorced, and if she has any children. Some tribes believe that the tattooed symbols provide protection from evil. He also shared that French colonial scholars, in their search for the origins of Berber art, suggested that North African Berber tattoos resembled Neolithic pictograms in caves in Spain.

Up until now, the Berbers had seemed delighted to have us in their midst but suddenly, a woman was yammering at me and wagging her finger in Andy's direction. The other women in the tent began nodding, concurring with her. We were obviously doing something wrong, but what? Driss was off helping his father trade horses and bargain for rifles, so we didn't have our translator to clarify why we were causing such a stir.

My gaze followed the direction of the women's pointing fingers and narrowed eyes, landing on Galen, who was in the pack on Andy's back. The women continued to *tsk*, poke and pull on my sleeve, pointing at Andy and Galen, empathically trying to tell me something.

Ahhh—the man should not be carrying the baby. That was my job.

They calmed down once we transferred Galen to my back, then gestured for us to sit on the rug and drink tea. It was an elaborate process that involved dramatically pouring scalding water in a high stream into the teapot over seven different kinds of herbs—wild mint, thyme, lemongrass, geranium, sage, verbena, and a hint of absinthe wormwood—and three or four generous clumps of raw sugar. Our hostess then put the teapot directly on the flame to bring it back to a boil.

After serving us the cloyingly sweet tea, the women went back to their chores, humming and murmuring softly to each other.

It was busy under the eaves of this open-sided tent. As I jiggled Galen on my lap, Andy and I watched bearded men sharpen daggers and scythes on whetstones; women in ornately embroidered black dresses trudged in, carrying amphorae of sloshing water on their backs; babies crawled over every faded orange, red, and green wool rug overlapped on the floor; and the older children stared in wonder at Galen's corn silk hair.

The next day we were invited to share a meal with Driss's extended clan. Aromas of greasy grilling lamb and savory tajines mingled with the sharp odor of camel dung, smoke, and dust that hung like a thick cloud throughout the tent.

One of Driss's distant cousins had the most gorgeous baby about Galen's size. She had huge doe eyes framed in kohl, eyelashes thick and black, mocha skin, and a wind-chime laugh. Engraved and beaded bracelets adorned her pudgy arms.

I admired the child and the mother held her beautiful

baby out for me to hold as I passed Galen to her.

Galen and the little girl clasped hands and were juxtaposed light and dark mirror images of plump infant cuteness.

The entire tribe gathered around, cooing over the two babies. We laughed and agreed how adorable they were together. They were even batting their eyes, flirting with each other.

The parents made playful, suggestive gestures about the two becoming engaged, and Driss said teasingly, "They think we should marry them here at Imilchil today when the governor flies in to officiate the group marriage ceremony. Everyone is exclaiming they are a perfect match."

Andy and I laughed and had to agree—our babies were a good-looking couple. Meanwhile, Galen was leaning toward his new girlfriend, trying to plant a gooey kiss and embrace her in a wobbly hug. She beamed and seemed amenable to this new-found baby love.

Curious, I said, "Driss, ask them what their child's name is."

The father proudly intoned, "Muhammad."

The parents then pointed to Galen, inquiring what "her" name was.

Uh oh. I froze, the sea of expectant, smiling faces making my face flush as though from a spotlight. "Um...his name...is... Muhammad...?"

The temperature in the tent grew frosty as the baby's mother and father grabbed little Muhammad from my arms and stalked off, deeply offended that we had mistaken their firstborn son for a lowly girl.

Driss pulled us out of the tent in a hurry without saying goodbye to his cousins, who were glowering at us from the back of the tent.

Once out of earshot, he said, "Well, that was embarrassing! Guess I will stay out of the marriage broker business. Let's pack up. We will leave right after the ceremony this afternoon."

In silence, we wandered to the epicenter of the festivities, where a large stage had been set up. Several dozen teenage couples in full ceremonial regalia shyly wandered through the crowd, holding hands. The young girls in a flurry of fabrics, headdresses, and jewelry; the young bucks—many shorter than their brides-to-be—in white shirts and pants, daggers dangling from their belts.

Galen slept soundly in the pack on my back, a blanket draped over his head to protect him from the high winds and also to ensure that he would not be mistaken for a marriageable girl-child.

Tribal flags snapped in the gusts. A helicopter buzzed across the valley and landed near the stage in a frenzy of clapping, vocal trilling, and the ubiquitous rifle fire.

The copter's rotary blades kicked up tornados of bone-dry silt, which hovered about the debarking governor like a mystical shroud. With great fanfare he brushed the dust off his satin baseball jacket and mounted the stage, holding a bullhorn. Over all the chaotic noise, he gave a speech and then announced that the couples were now man and wife. And that was it. Very anti-climactic. Everyone dispersed, Andy and I scribbled a few notes for our travel piece we'd work on during the flight home, and Driss herded us back to the jeep, as he was in a hurry to catch his flight home to

Paris that evening.

Back at the hotel in Fez, Driss helped us load our mammoth pile of baby items into the rental car. Saying goodbye, he reached out to hold Galen, gave him a squeeze, and bounced him up and down. Galen grasped Driss's thumb and sucked on it. Gazing into my son's lake-blue eyes, Driss solemnly said, "Little Muhammad, I really enjoyed meeting you. I hope my son will be brave and strong, but not as pretty as you."

# EPILOGUE

A Berber musician friend of mine recently looked mystified when I asked him what "Willy Muhammad" meant and described the scene thirty years ago in the Atlas when Galen was prince of the tent show. I yelled it just like I remember the mustachioed chieftain doing as he hefted Galen above his head for the throngs of turbaned Berbers to admire. Puzzled, Khaled scratched his balding head and then said, "No, no. They must have been saying something like '*Wahedlee Muhammad*,' not 'Willy,' silly! It means, 'Oh, little Muhammad!'"

# TRUMPETS OF WARNING

Kenya 1987

Waking early our first full day at Little Governors'
Camp in the Maasai Mara Reserve in Kenya, we were
startled to see elephant, hippo, and warthog tracks circling
close to the edges of our canvas tent. Was that also a lion's
paw print inches from the tent flap?

The camp was unfenced with the guest tents and
dining hall situated around a large, popular waterhole.
The freshly made tracks around our tent were evidence
that the wildlife came and went through camp at all hours
of the day and night. Andy, my husband, and I were
warned not to walk anywhere unescorted and to zip our
tent up tight every time we departed so that the
proprietary troop of baboons would not enter and steal
stuff. They were partial to toothpaste and film canisters,
judging from their raid of the tent next to us the day

113

before.

As we left the tent, shivering in the pre-dawn chill, whistling announced we had company. A tall, young Maasai warrior bedecked in bold primary-colored beaded necklaces and shirtless with only a red cloth, called a *matavuvale,* wrapped around his narrow hips, was waiting outside our tent. A vintage silver coffee service was balanced on one palm, and slung over his shoulder was an antique Winchester rifle. He announced in an oddly soft voice, "My name is Nchaama. I am here to guard you." Galen, our four-year-old son, stared with saucer eyes as Nchaama towered over him, pouring coffee and hot chocolate into bone-white porcelain cups. Faint music emanated from his body. Walkman wires wound through his plaited hair and looped around his extended earlobes that grazed his shoulders. The song keening from the headphones was a classic: "Jumpin' Jack Flash."

While we savored our steaming drinks, Nchaama stood silently nearby, balanced on one foot. The other rested against his inner thigh. His smallish head bobbed to the Stones. Then, in a deep melodic voice he stated, "You are not allowed to go anywhere without an armed escort— that is me. Even from your tent to the dining hall." Andy raised his eyebrows as I felt my heart beat faster. We had picked this walk-in safari camp because of its unique isolation, accessible only by small plane, jeep, then a boat ride to the trail that led to the camp. Andy and I did not expect a private armed guard and wild animals right outside our tent!

Nchaama looked off into the distance, the entire time not wavering, even though he was still standing with only

114

one foot planted on the ground. Slowly, he looked down at us in our canvas camp chairs, shook his head at our naïveté, and said, "Two weeks before you arrived, a woman was gored by a cape buffalo who was peeved that she was on *his* trail." He continued the litany of dangers, saying, "Never, never stand on the river bank close to the water's edge. A tourist disappeared down there. We think a Nile crocodile lunged out of the water, knocked him over with its giant tail, and pulled him into the river. He is now stuffed under a log rotting somewhere. And the crocodile is eating him. They have very bad breath!"

This regal, slip-thin man who had been so animated, who smelled faintly of blood-rich game meat and sour milk, withdrew into silence again. As we continued to chew on freshly baked buttery scones, we were also digesting the multifarious dangers that could befall us on our family vacation. Disneyland this was not!

Suddenly, Nchaama sprung into action and collected our dishes, which would have been annoying, as we hadn't finished breakfast, but didn't matter since we had lost our appetites. With one bony, hooked finger he beckoned us to gather our gear and follow him. With no small amount of trepidation we fell into step, trying to keep up with his long-limbed stride. Like most tourists on safari we were loaded down with video gear, decked out in tan-colored jackets with row upon row of pockets crammed with film canisters, candy bars, water, and sunscreen. I felt like a walking Walgreens in a Banana Republic safari outfit.

The footpath wound through camp and skirted the waterhole where hippos floated, submerged, with nostrils poking above the waterline like rubbery periscopes. We tiptoed and whispered because hippos have a reputation of being easily annoyed and a cantankerous lot with a mean bite when they decide to sink their thick teeth into you. Plus, they can run really fast—like an out-of-control linebacker on stubby legs. Something I did not want to witness this early in the morning.

We got past the watering hole in one piece and headed into the dense bush. White-bellied Go-away-birds and Lilac-breasted Rollers heralded the rising sun. The cool air quickly evaporated as the sun glinted higher and the light grew sharper.

Galen held my hand and chirped questions in a singsong happy trill. "Where are the giraffes?" he asked. It thrilled him that his stuffed toys at home in California had morphed into super-sized, real-life African animals. When we had flown into Little Governors' Camp from Nairobi the day before in a Cessna, a large herd of giraffes dramatically draped in caramel-colored spots were startled by the plane's engine thrum and galloped, legs akimbo, down the dirt runway. They moved like mechanical toys.

Nchaama and Andy walked ahead of us on the trail. A trumpeting from deep within the canopy broke the morning avian cacophony. The bushes rattled just a few yards away from us on the side of the trail. Then, another loud trumpet blast blew the branches apart like a theater curtain and an African savanna elephant poked his head from the green wall, flapped his sail-sized ears in our direction, and raised his trunk in yet another and even more urgent warning. He stood defiantly a stone's throw distance away on the left side of the trail.

"Run, run!" Nchaama shouted.

Maasai, who have very long legs, are known for their Olympic track medals. Much to my surprise, Andy was on his heels, having dropped the video equipment to bolt forward after Nchaama in a champion sprint. They both disappeared down the trail, leaving Galen and me to fend for ourselves.

My feet were frozen to the ground and I gripped Galen's hand tightly. He was preoccupied with a glossy horned rhinoceros beetle crawling on the trail in front of him, completely unconcerned about the elephant's threatening attitude or proximity. I glanced surreptitiously at the elephant, avoiding eye contact. He glowered directly at me. His great bulk seethed as he stomped his large padded feet, put his head down, and charged at us. I scooped up my son and the camera gear bag and flew helter-skelter down the path. The pachyderm's thunderous pounding grew louder as he gained speed and closed the gap between us.

Galen giggled and pointed back at the elephant in glee as he jostled up and down on my hip with every stride. He thought this was a game of chase. Just as I was about to drop the gear in order to run faster and keep a tight grip on my squirming son, the trail turned a bend and there was the riverbank. Nchaama and my husband were already perched in the skiff, ready to shove off. They waved me on with encouraging cheers. "Come on, you can do it! Watch out for the crocodiles!" They yelled and slapped their thighs. Did they think this was some kind of circus relay?

I plopped Galen and myself into the boat with no help

from either of the men. My heart pounded. My face was red. I was a sweaty mess pumped up on adrenaline. And I was really pissed off.

The bull elephant had stopped his chase and stood a ways off looking at us, slowly flapping his ears. Then, he nonchalantly sauntered back into the bushes. "He is heading to the garbage cans now," Nchaama said in a casual tone that insinuated this survival race was a daily occurrence.

I swiveled around and took a good, long, and reassessing look at Andy. He was chatting with Nchaama as if nothing had happened. Doubts about his parental instincts swirled around my mind. I vowed not to talk to him for the rest of the day.

Nachaama maneuvered the skiff past a few floating hippos and we were dropped off on the other side of the Mara River where a jeep idled. Nchaama (who I was also not speaking to) introduced us to our personal guide and driver for the next five days of our safari. He was short and round with very different features than the Maasai. He seemed aloof as he introduced himself. "My name is Josef. I am Kikuyu." The Kikuyu are Kenya's largest ethnic group and rivals of the Maasai.

We had specifically requested Josef because his reputation was unsurpassed. What Josef lacked in personality and charm he made up for in an uncanny ability to pinpoint the location of the game animals on any given day. This was crucial. A typical safari could take hours and hours of driving over the savanna with nary a critter in sight.

The Maasai Mara Reserve is the size of Rhode Island

and the animals roam freely throughout. It was obvious each night during dinner which guests had had sightings that day. Their conversations were animated as they chittered and chattered excitedly about lions and cheetahs, zebras, hyenas, even rhinos. Then there were the sullen, quiet tables—guests who'd endured the all-day dusty jeep treks with little wildlife. It was hard to witness their postured disappointment in the candlelit dining hall as their somber, elongated shadows wavered on the taupe fabric tent walls.

Josef also turned out to be the driver for the stars and had just spent a week with Mick Jagger, Jerry Hall, and their kids. Mick hadn't cared about seeing the wildlife. He had requested Josef to drive them far away from people and even lions, park under a shade tree, mix martinis, and lay out picnics while the family played card games undisturbed.

Josef emanated a keen dislike for tourists, but took a shine to Galen and invited him to sit in the front of the jeep, leaving Andy and me bumping along the rutted tracks on the springless back seat. Fortunately, our son was oblivious to my simmering unhappiness as I mulled over the elephant incident. He joyfully sang ditties he made up about the animals—the highlight being when we encountered a pride of lions lying about like a plush wildcat carpet, sultans and sultanas sated after a kill. Galen stood on the seat, holding onto the lowered window, leaned out, and crooned an improvised lullaby to the lions in an angelic, unselfconscious child's voice. The lions swiveled their heads toward us in the shimmering midday heat, perked up their ears and...grinned. Josef shook his head in disbelief and said with unusual zest, "I have never seen the lions smile or had anybody sing to them. Even Mick Jagger!" From that moment on, Galen sat on Josef's lap and steered the jeep across the vast savanna plain, both of them humming and crooning away as if Andy and I weren't in the vehicle with them.

The ornery bull elephant never made another appearance during our daily half-mile tromp on the trail from the camp to the river, but his trumpeted warnings continued to ring in my head.

By our last day, I was almost used to the snuffling and snorting of animals milling about, checking out our tent at night, though their inquisitive noises invaded my sleep. Giant animals paraded through my dreamscape bellowing and roaring.

Our five-day safari was over. Nchaama escorted us one last time to the riverbank and waved goodbye. The dinghy floated us across the river, avoiding the floating rumps and heads of the hippos, where Josef waited in the jeep to drive us to the airstrip. He lingered with us in the shade of a lone Shepherd's Tree while he and Galen drew animals in the red dust with a crooked stick as we waited for the plane to appear on the horizon. A bruised silence hung between Andy and me in the stiflingly hot, dry air.

As we boarded the plane, Josef hugged Galen and said, "You *must* return. I will show you how to be a safari guide and you will teach me the animal songs." He then lifted Galen up to me before the pilot closed the door. I sat a few seats away from Andy. The Cessna's propellers spun faster and faster as we lofted into the relentless blue sky. From the tiny plane window the landscape shimmered and undulated in the heat. Below us, the awkward-legged giraffes scattered in all directions.

# POLKA DOT BIKINI

Belize 1994

I once had an hourglass figure that could sport bikinis. My most sexy suit was a black and white polka dot number that fit like a glove and made the curves look even curvier. Not only did I think this suit was hot, but men did, too.

Not only men, but males of another species took a gander when I'd swim in this particular suit. I had no idea dolphins were fashionistas until one holiday visit to Anthony's Key Resort on Roatan in the Bay Islands of Honduras, where my husband, son, and I had stayed over many Christmas holidays. Scuba diving was the main attraction, as the world's second-longest barrier reef system lies just off Roatan's shores, providing some of the best diving in the Caribbean.

There is also a dolphin research station run by the Roatan Institute for Marine Sciences on nearby Bailey's Key. It supports itself by allowing guests to swim with the dolphins for a fee, after a brief orientation by one of the trainers.

My young son enjoyed these frolicking encounters, as the dozen Atlantic bottlenose dolphins were usually playful and friendly. The bottlenose dolphin is common in the Caribbean, and is rather large. They range in size from 6 feet to 14 feet, and their body is smooth like rubbery soapstone with a grey-blue patina that is pleasing to touch when they allow physical contact. The most outstanding feature are their expressive eyes, which can emanate a wide range of messages from a twinkly, whimsical invitation to play to a deep, yearning gaze that begs connection, or the complete opposite—a glowering warning to keep your distance.

We'd been on dolphin swims at the research station many times during our vacations at Anthony's, and each interaction was different. One time an adult female glided into my arms and flopped over, allowing me to rock her as she gazed languidly into my eyes. On another swim, a female dolphin grabbed Galen, my son, by the wrist with her teeth and tried to swim off with him. He was 6 years old and this frightened him. He felt he was being kidnapped and taken deeper into her watery realm against his will. It took a bit of coaxing to get her to leave him alone, and after a few tears were shed, Galen entered the water again and had fun throwing balls to the young males.

The next year we returned to Anthony's as usual. In

my suitcase was my hot new bikini that I was a bit self-conscious about wearing, but I also kind of felt like strutting my stuff. Closing in on 40 years old does this to a woman.

We dove with the rainbow parrotfish and whitetip reef sharks during the day, and with the octopuses and spiny lobsters at night. On New Year's Eve I danced on the bar top, doing the windey-windey taught to me by a spunky teenage Honduran girl. The windey-windey is a dance that can get you pregnant. The hips are isolated and around and around they rapidly circle as you gyrate your way down the polished mahogany bar in an ecstatic Caribbean conga line of happy dancers. It is hella good fun—unless you take a nosedive off the bar and break your neck (which, thankfully, nobody did due to our limber state of mind). Like I mentioned, mid-life crisis.

We stayed up till dawn limboing our way into the new year. Even my young son got dance lessons from the adorable teenage girl. Scuba diving was out of the question the following day—headaches do not mix well with deep diving. So we went for our annual dolphin swim at the research station.

I donned the polka dot bikini and felt slightly confident when I looked in the mirror and perused my still-shapely body in the snazzy suit.

Galen brought an underwater camera to photograph his marine mammal friends, many of whom he knew by name. After the introductory etiquette talk by the naturalist that we could, by this point, quote almost word-for-word, we waded into the gin-clear water with six other guests, avid scuba divers like us taking a break from

125

diving after our New Year's Eve hoopla.

At first, there was no sign of our finny friends, so we stood in the shallows waiting to see what would happen. Suddenly, the water was turbulent. The entire pod frenetically circled me and then swam away. Again, the dolphins rushed straight at me and this time, the largest male chased the others away. He swam up close, lifting his steel-grey-blue face out of the water. He looked me in the eye and grinned. A really big, goofy grin. The other dolphins hung back, not socializing with any of the other people in the water.

I stared at him, wondering what was up with his faux stretched-out smile when he dipped down and swam against my legs, almost knocking me over. I regained my balance and he intentionally bumped into me again. He circled, and rubbed against me. This was kind of fun. He felt cool, solid, and smooth. It was amusing. Until it hurt. Suddenly, his smooth skin had a razor-like edge to it. I looked down and he was now sideways against me, and there was something oblong protruding from his belly. It was about 10 inches in length and pointed. And rough like sandpaper. Could it be? Why yes—it was a dolphin dick!

Then things really heated up. As he enthusiastically humped my leg, the female dolphins decided their homeboy was paying way too much attention to the wrong female. They rushed directly at me in a tight group, heads out of the water, pointy teeth displayed, and made a racketous, chittering noise in unison as they charged. Now I was alarmed. I knew a jealous female when I saw one—it didn't matter what species! They stopped a few inches from my chest, glowered at me, and then backed up with their tails and did it all over again. I felt like I was in a *Flipper* porn flick drama. I froze, cornered by the male, who simply ignored his harem's choreographed terror attack on me while busy trying to impregnate my thighs.

A shrill, piercing sound broke the spell. The trainer stood on the beach blowing his whistle hard and fast, yelling, "Everyone out of the water NOW!" I batted away my hard-on friend—and his agitated harem—then stumbled out of the water and onto the beach. Everyone else, including my husband and son, stood there gaping at me. No one asked if I was all right; they just stared. Looking down, I noticed my bathing suit was completely askew. Not only had *Señor* Randy Fish been getting a rub-on on my leg, he had also practically de-suited me. What a masterful horndog! This 12-foot-long male marine mammal took me right back to my high school years and the reason I avoided drive-in movies.

"I have never seen them behave this way!" exclaimed the flustered trainer. "I'm giving you all refunds as this is the first time I've ever canceled a dolphin swim experience." He then looked directly at me, gave me the once-over, and pointedly said, "I guess in the future I will have to request that guests not wear polka dot bikinis."

## AUTHOR'S NOTE

I have come to realize it is wrong to keep dolphins, or any wild animals, in captivity. I believe dolphins should swim freely in the oceans with their family pods and not be forced to live in isolation in aquariums, theme parks, zoos, and hotels with "dolphin swims". No creature should have to leap through flaming hoops or swim backward on its tail to get fed. Join me in boycotting all venues where animals are held in captivity to entertain humans. Find out more at www.dolphinproject.org

# RUNNING WITH WOLVES IN THE NEGEV

Israel 1998

We jounce along the crater floor in the pitch black of night. I am annoyed.

"Why won't you tell me where we're going?" My displeasure escapes like a hiss from a pressure cooker.

We've been driving in the dark for hours, and I have no idea where we are or why. It's another one of Adir's "adventures." I had envisioned a romantic beachside getaway, and this was certainly not the beach.

He is so infuriating and such an Israeli! He was born a *Sabra*, which, literally translated, means "prickly pear"—a thorny desert plant with thick skin that conceals a sweet, softer interior. The term is used to describe a Jew born in Palestine or, after 1948, in Israel. Adir is the classic tough-yet-sensitive-and-very-stubborn man-child of the Promised Land.

Adir is also a pain in the ass. An attractive, sexy, twenty-years-younger-than-me pain in the ass.

He pays no attention to my irritable mood and leans forward over the steering wheel, careening through the dust clouds that veil the dirt road. Barely keeping us on the track, he grins like an Evel Knievel demon-driver.

How does he know of this place, this ancient crater in the Negev Desert, once the floor of a primordial sea, still sprinkled with a delicate layer of marine snail shells?

The word *negev* is derived from a Hebrew word meaning "dry." Shadowy shapes of an occasional acacia tree rise from the arid soil, but other than that, the Negev is a desert with no sand, just rock and dirt. The rocks exposed are from the Triassic period, 250 million years ago. This place is the innards of the earth. And we are going to camp here.

Determined to surprise me with all the hidden quarters of Israel, Adir swept me up when I arrived in Tel Aviv for a two-week tryst and proceeded to whisk me into every recess of this enigmatic and tumultuous land. Forget Jerusalem, Bethlehem, Eilat, or Haifa. Instead, we traveled to remote, stark, and hostile places clothed in thorns and parched geography inhabited only by night creatures like wolves, owls, and voles—not any places a normal tourist would visit or humans would live.

"Whoa!" Adir yells as he slams on the brakes and we skid sideways.

Ridged, furry backs and low-slung hips on sinewy legs slalom in front of our weaving headlights. Crazy yellow eyes glinting, tongues hanging, it's a pack of wild

Arabian wolves. They lope ahead of us for a timeless moment, then veer off into the brush to hunt in the dark obscurity of a moonless night.

Adir parks and announces, "Here we will camp."

A biting chill snaps at my skin. I had not packed for a camping trip. It's hot in the Middle East. No jacket, no boots, no hat, no gloves. Just a floral sundress, big-eyed sunglasses, strappy sandals, and a polka dot bikini. At forty-five years old I can still pull this off—despite a sixteen-year-old son and a passion for pasta.

Thick carpets of stars glitter and spark, taunting me to stay awake and witness their pageantry. This is not difficult as I am freezing my butt off in the Negev.

Adir pulls a scratchy blanket out from the back of the truck and lays it down on the hard, cold ground. Our bedroll. No cover for warmth. No pillows for comfort. No tent to protect us from wolves running wild. They can smell warm blood; ours is still warm. Sort of.

Why worry—I am with the original lone wolf. He has a thick mane of glossy black hair that I love to pull, gleaming agate eyes that hold my gaze, and a huge appetite for meat—mine. He bites my neck, nips my thighs. Adir snarls at other men who look my way, and he protected me from Syrian landmines on the Golan Heights border on one of our many forays to the boundaries of this intense region. He feeds me spicy home-cooked meals and scrubs me down in his makeshift shower when we return late and dusty from hikes up the *wadis* in Ein Gedi where he resides. He is my protector, guide, and lover.

How did I meet this wiry-haired, reckless Sabra?

Six months earlier, kayaking on a spring runoff river

in California, I was about to pull my boat onto the beach when he strode into the icy water, lifted me out of the kayak—to the astonishment of the other rafters—and carried me to shore. Not a drop of water touched my skin. His warm hands clasped me firmly to his bare, glistening chest.

I had scarcely given him a hello when I met him the day before, even though he never stopped staring at me, but now he forced me to acknowledge him as I reclined there, astonished, in his well-muscled arms.

He was the chef on a rafting expedition I was a guide for. I did not know his name on that incendiary day on the banks of the Kings River, yet he devoured me with his eyes and then with his mouth as he closed it against mine. His lips were hot, soft, and insistent.

His luscious kisses caused me to ignite and collide—irresistibly pressing my flesh against his. I wanted his flaming lips to brand me. This man was passion incarnate.

An eternity passed as heat waves shimmered off the scalding sand. It was 100 degrees midday. He was barefoot yet immune to the burning beach.

Suddenly aware that everyone around us seemed suspended in place by this seductive scene, my hands, which cupped his face, dropped. I pounded my fists against his chest, fell to the sand, and ran back out into the freezing snowmelt river to cool down.

I tried to ignore him the rest of the trip. His zeal and relentless ardor alarmed and confounded me. I'd be walking from my tent to the makeshift kitchen and he would reach from behind an oak tree and pull me toward him like a striking rattlesnake. Startled, I'd find myself bent backward in the throes of a Rhett Butler smooch, lip-locking until I caught my breath, and my senses, and then shoved him away. The third time he tried to steal a kiss, I slapped him. Hard. I was tired of his antics. I had a job to do teaching people how to run these big boat-eating rapids, and there was no energy or time left for romance.

He sure could cook, but his refreshing mint and cucumber tabouli salads didn't cool his passions. His coal-black eyes burned into me as he flipped latkes or chopped onions. It's amazing he didn't slice off a finger with one of his razor-sharp chef knives.

I spent a lot of time in my kayak that Kings River trip. Just far enough offshore that he couldn't nab me. The other rafting guides thought my avoidance of Romeo was funny, and would tease him till he blushed and waved knives in their faces.

I wasn't going to get involved with some kid twenty years younger than me who lived in Israel and was in California on a working holiday. Who had no control over his libido or impulses. No way. Though he was kinda cute. Okay, downright gorgeous—and I already knew he could kiss like a devil on steroids.

After the river trip ended, he rented a room from a mutual friend in the same town where I lived, and he called me daily. I had not given him my phone number. He left abrupt messages asking me out on dinner dates, each one an iteration of, "You will go out to dinner with me!" pronounced more like a command than a question. He persisted for two weeks, even though I never called him back...until one night.

One night when I was really pissed off at the man I

had been dating for the past year—let's call him "Mr. Waffley." This guy was a psychotherapist and afraid of commitment. I didn't want commitment; I wanted roses, a lip lock, hot sex, and romance and let's face it: it's not romantic when you're thick in an embrace and he pulls away and says, "Sometimes I love you, and sometimes I don't."

Enough of that. I called Adir in the wee morning hours of that one night. I knew he would answer, even though it was 3 a.m.

He must have driven at warp speed to arrive at my doorstep just 10 minutes after I hung up. And he never left. No waffling either—just you-know-what. Lots of it. For weeks, until he had to return to Israel.

We went to Burning Man and burned.

He cooked my mom a birthday feast.

He sold my son his beater car.

It delighted me when I heard noises in the kitchen in the middle of the night. It was not a burglar—it was Adir concocting *shakshouka*, a savory Israeli dish of saffron, paprika, and parsley flavoring tomatoes, bell peppers, onions, and fried eggs, all served with tahini sauce and pita bread.

This man had a beastly appetite and it was contagious. As he chopped, sautéed, and stirred we'd have sex against the butcher block table. The hanging skillets swayed and clanked. My moans reverberated against the plates quivering on the countertop. We'd wash it all down with bold red wine, then take a moonlit stroll, holding hands in the pre-dawn stillness.

But then he packed up his knives and flew back to

Israel. We agreed not to continue our romance long-distance.

But I could not keep the agreement. Nor could he.

We called each other weekly. The phone lines crackled with desire despite the distance of continents and cultures.

A few months later, I traveled to his country. I had hitchhiked through Israel for three months in 1973, but it had changed dramatically since my last visit. There were roadblocks with soldiers sporting Uzis every few miles on our way south.

Our first night at his kibbutz in Ein Gedi, on the western edge of the Dead Sea, we had dinner with his family. They were yelling in Hebrew at each other across the dinner table. I whispered to Adir, "Why are they arguing?" Confused, he shook his head and responded, "They are just asking for someone to pass them the butter, or the bread, or the salt."

I sat back in shock, my ears ringing from the commotion. My family spoke in soft, civilized tones while engaging in pleasant dinner conversation. The one time my mom raised her voice at my dad at the dinner table, I was convinced they were getting a divorce.

The next day Adir would not come with me to Jerusalem. He said, "You go by yourself. There are too many guns and soldiers." I had no idea what he was talking about. I had lived in the Old City of Jerusalem for a month on that first adventure and found it a very friendly place, showcasing delicious chickpea hummus served with oven-hot puffy pita bread on rooftops of Palestinian hotels, and poppy-seed *hamantash* cookies, which I ate with old Jewish bank guards who'd befriend me on my way back to the hostel. Fat Hasidic women scrubbed my back in the *hammam* on the days women were allowed to go to the public bathhouse. After scalding steam baths, these girthy women lounged about, eating oranges and pastries while massaging each other. They had included the skinny California girl in their circle of sisterhood of snacking, rubbing, and gossiping.

This time I found Jerusalem a cold and fearful place. Soldiers carrying machine guns met me around every corner. Security barriers surrounded the Dome of the Rock mosque and the Wailing Wall, and the Arab merchants were twitchy and rude in the souk. The sidewalks were crowded with orthodox Hasidic settlers from America, their accents giving them away as I walked past. No one made eye contact or said hello to me. Adir was right. Jerusalem was no place to linger.

Returning from another one of our mystery tours, this one to the Golan Heights, we drove through the ultra-conservative Hasidic section of Jerusalem on the Sabbath. Brow furrowed, Adir raced through all the red lights. When I demanded to know why we were dangerously barrel-assing through Jerusalem, he said in a terrorized tone that I had never heard him speak in before, "They will stone us if they see us driving on the Sabbath!" That was when I noticed we were the only people in the sole moving vehicle on the street, even though it was the middle of the day.

He wouldn't drive me to Jericho, either, claiming it was impossible to visit, which turned out to be true. Israel prohibited Jews from entering Jericho, as it is in Palestinian territory on the West Bank.

I thought I could walk in like I had in 1973 since I wasn't Jewish, so the restriction might not apply to me. But Adir was horrified so I dropped the idea, though my heart ached at not being able to visit the oldest town on Earth populated by some of the most hospitable people I had ever encountered.

Surrounded by barbed-wire walls, police checkpoints, and a two-meter-wide trench, the ancient city of Jericho had the trappings of a prison camp doused in misery and rage. Not the peaceful, idyllic Palestinian village I had lingered in for two weeks twenty-six years ago, when orange groves and the banks of the Jordan River were the only boundaries surrounding it.

He did take me to the wild, unpopulated places. And it was in the wild, unpopulated, damned cold crater in the Negev, as I tried to get comfortable on our bedroll while wolves paced around us just beyond eyesight, that I truly began to witness the complicated and wounded side of Adir.

He was at peace in the solitude of nature. It wasn't long before I began to realize, here in the stillness of life untouched, that Adir sought silence for healing while I sought dialog for understanding.

He was infuriating because he would suddenly stop talking in mid-sentence. It might be hours before a word passed his lips. No kisses, either. Instead of bridling with passion, he brooded, retreating to the lair in his mind.

What was going on in there? Was he a genius or a nut job?

His vast silences shut me out. I felt lonely. I'd go for walks by myself in the arid wilderness, wondering why I had traveled so far to spend time with a man who would not articulate his feelings except in bed.

After one particularly tortured mute sulk that made me consider getting on the next plane home, he started to speak. He sat smoking under a date palm, his back to me, gazing out over the hazy Dead Sea. Across the saline waters the shores of the Kingdom of Jordan were faintly outlined in the sunlight along the sea's edge.

He said, "I fought in Lebanon. I was only eighteen years old. Horrible things happened there and I was part of it."

I had no idea he'd been conscripted, and remained quiet while he blew smoke rings. He continued. "Being drafted into the military is considered a rite of passage in Israel. Men serve three years, women two years. Then we continue as reservists into our fifties, getting called for training and active duty for over a month annually."

I stroked his hair as he muttered, "I must figure out a way to never fight again—to become a war resistor. Even if it means I claim insanity. I have been thinking long about it." Adir wiped the back of his hand against his wet cheek and said, "This will be very difficult as I'll be ostracized and the chances of getting a job will be slim. The officials will try to make my life unbearable."

The tremor in his voice lessened and his back straightened as he told his story—one that I'd only gathered bits and pieces of until now. "I am a true Sabra—born in Israel. My parents are Yemenite Jews. They were airlifted here in 1949 to populate the new state of Israel in a mass migration program called Operation Magic Carpet. They were promised a kibbutz in a fertile region, but were posted to a tent camp on the Lebanese border in a barren area with no development funds. I grew up hungry, with bombs and landmines in the school playground. Going into the army was awful, too, because I was treated like a second-class citizen due to my darker skin."

Now I understood his pained silences. He was serving a country that had made broken promises to his parents and treated him like dirt. The war had changed him. Killing people wounded him. Like many vets, he did not talk about it. Until he met me. I didn't glorify military service and believed it is a soul-killer to hand a young person a gun and tell him or her to point it at "the enemy." I was humbled that he knew me well enough to trust that I could listen without judgment of his mutiny and encourage him to follow his heart.

We talked past sunset into the darkness. His inconsolable sadness floated out across the moonlight shimmering on the still sea. No sex, just dialog on our last night together.

The next day I flew back to California, both of us knowing it was our final rendezvous. I would never relocate to Israel, or convert to Judaism, and he would never live far from his family. I did not want any more children; he did.

He never did take me to a beach resort. My sundress was torn, stained with mineraly earth as I boarded the plane back to San Francisco, my suitcase stuffed with spices—paprika, zatar, cumin, and saffron.

At the airport, before we parted, Adir gave me one last lingering kiss and then handed me a gift-wrapped package. I crammed it into my carry-on, only to have it confiscated minutes later at customs. The vigilant security officials ripped the wrapping off, and nestled in the box was a Henckels fully forged chef's knife, which they promptly bagged, tagged, and addressed.

Surprisingly, it made it to San Francisco.

Over the next few months, he called frequently to talk about his plan to extricate himself from the mandatory military service imposed upon his people. I listened carefully, aware that I was the only person he could talk to about this.

"I'm going to claim insanity, but no one in my family can know I'm doing it intentionally. After all, my brother works for Mossad—the secret police—in Tel Aviv."

"Adir, please don't drive yourself over the edge. Take care of yourself. I'm worried about you," I pleaded, pressing the phone against my ear with my shoulder as I stirred pinches of the Israeli spices into a lamb stew for my family's dinner that night.

To instigate his plan, Adir did not eat. He did not bathe. He did not sleep for days on end. He drank gallons of acid-black coffee. He smoked unfiltered cigarettes. His chiseled face overgrew with a scraggly beard. He purposely journeyed to the blurry mindscape of mental illness. The psychiatrists had to be convinced. It took months.

In one of his many interviews with them, he said, "I do not know what I will do if you put a gun in my hand again. I do not know which way I will point it." The psychiatric evaluators thought he meant shooting at his own troops, but when Adir told me of this, I knew he meant shooting himself to avoid fighting. The phone shook in my hand and tears welled, but all I could do was listen as he shared his troubled unraveling.

After yet another session in which the psychiatrist challenged Adir's masculinity, Adir called me from his parents' kibbutz on the Lebanese border. Laughing, his vocal chords strained like a tightrope, he said, "I might come to California."

To distract him from his impulse to run away, I asked, "Are you working?"

"I got a chef job at a resort in Eilat but it didn't work out," he said in a monotone. "They didn't appreciate my improvisational style...especially with spices."

He laughed halfheartedly. "I do my best cooking in the middle of the night for sexy, wild women."

Listening to the despair in his voice, I glanced upward at the silent skillets hanging above the stove, reminiscing with a twinge of longing Adir's passionate way of combining sex and cooking, feeling his lips on my neck, my cheeks, my lips.

"You should be dating. Find a woman who wants to camp with you in the Negev. Who loves your cooking. Have a family. You will be a great dad."

A long sigh came across the phone lines. "That won't happen. These Israeli girls don't like dark-skinned cowards."

Fifteen years later, I use the Henckels knife to mince pungent herbs from my garden—marjoram, thyme, oregano, rosemary, chives, basil. I keep the blade razor sharp.

Sometimes, out of the corner of my vision, I see the hungry gleam of Adir's eyes glinting in the carbon steel.

I hope his wounds are healed and there is laughter and joy in his crazy wolf eyes. I pray he has not been left howling alone in the Negev in the dark.

# SLEEPING ON SEKHMET

Italy 2001

"*Per favore*, call me Platypus," said the be-spectacled, caftan-clad receptionist in a lilting Italian accent. He pronounced it "Plaah-tee-puuhz." Charming when he said it but it did not roll off my tongue.

"We have our own currency, so please change your dollars into Damanhurian coins at the machine behind you. You can use your ATM card."

This Platypus man was very polite while giving me these odd instructions, but before I could collect my room key he exclaimed, "*Rapido! Rapido!* Set your suitcase behind my desk. You can join the British sidekick ladies' tour to the museum, but get on that purple bus waiting outside right *now*."

Now I was really confused—I think he meant

"psychic," not "sidekick," and I didn't know I was supposed to go on a tour. My growling stomach also reminded me I hadn't eaten yet today. For the first time, I questioned my decision to write a story for my monthly travel column about this tiny but famous Italian commune of Damanhur where people with weird animal names meandered by wearing flowing robes.

Platypus hurriedly shuffled me onto the bus, which was packed full of chatty Brits. I was delegated to a seat in the back next to a rosy-cheeked older woman wearing a robin-egg-blue straw hat. A silk sunflower was tucked in the hatband.

"Why, an American! How *very* charming," she announced loudly in a Julia Child accent to the other ladies in the bus, who all swiveled and greeted me in jolly unison. "Hello, we are psychics from England on a spiritual holiday."

They absolutely adored that I was from San Francisco. "It is a hotbed of psychics and tarot readers. We all want to go there someday. Tell us all about flower power and hippies."

Pondering what to say about my hometown, the busty little lady next to me in the blue straw hat held out a metal cookie tin and said, "Dearie, have a biscuit."

The purple bus bumped along through the rocky green foothills of Piedmont in the northernmost province of Italy on a crisp fall day. Chewing on the delectable buttery shortbread biscuits, I marveled that just this morning I'd been on a train from Bologna where I'd taught a dance workshop.

Multi-job-tasking, I had arrived at Damanhur for a

three-day stay to research a story about this spiritual eco-community named after an ancient subterranean Egyptian temple meaning "City of Light."

The psychic Brits were handing me biscuits faster than I could eat them, asking personal questions in chirpy voices, and beaming at me affectionately.

"Oooh, you are a dance teacher and a writer. You will have to join us for the blindfolded goddess dance workshop tomorrow."

I was being adopted by this gaggle of grandmothers next to whom I was beginning to feel a bit staid compared to their all-embracing enthusiasm for cosmic New Age activities. Still munching on those mouthwatering cookies, and *still* trying to figure out how I had been swept into their psychic circus, I didn't notice we had entered the city of Turin and the bus had parked in a cobblestone alley shadowed from the noontime rays.

The bus driver and tour guide explained, "We parked behind the Museum of Egyptian Antiquities so that you can enter the Hall of Memory through the secret door."

A wave of murmurs rose from the ladies. "Oh, a secret entrance! How perfect," whispered my seatmate and biscuit provisioner.

We were escorted through two massive oak doors that groaned loudly as if in protest when they were pushed open. I was a half-head taller than my busload of new best friends and could see over their silvery hair into a dimly-lit hall streaked with dancing dust motes.

"I am your curator." Seeming to appear out of nowhere, a baritone voice boomed from a tall, dignified man wearing a midnight-blue tailored Italian suit. The

145

ladies huddled together; several tittered nervously, and all peered at him attentively.

He arched his silver eyebrows and continued, "You have just entered through the door that is always open. We never lock it. Secret to the public, mostly, but known by others in the occult communities who come here to reflect and walk the Hall of Memory."

Odd, I didn't know there was an Egyptian Museum outside of Cairo, except for the collection at the British Museum. I'd been to Egypt twice and I'd never heard of a "Hall of Memory." This was beginning to have the Masonic tone of a Dan Brown novel with a soupçon of gothic Anne Rice.

With the air of a stylish Oxfordian scholar, our guide rocked on his heels and said, "This museum has the second-largest Egyptian collection in the world. In the 1800s, the Italians were leading the pack in archeological digs in Egypt funded by the Dukes of Savoy, whose residence was Turin. The bounty was brought back to their private collection, which is now housed here."

We shuffled into a drafty room lined with fingerprint-smudged glass display cases filled with relics. And another room filled with more sooty, indiscernible objects. None were labeled and our guide swept past them, giving them a cursory wave of his hand and mumbled explanations. The smell in the museum was reminiscent of the musty spices of an Egyptian souk, but silent without the insistent vendors and throng of *galabia*-wearing shoppers.

The curator came to an abrupt halt in front of one of the cases and pointed to a small, nondescript artifact.

Solemnly he said, "Falco, the founder of Damanhur, came to the museum every Sunday with his father when he was growing up. On one visit, he cast his gaze on this piece. It gripped him in a hypnotic trance where he was swept back in time and shown all of his past lives. From that moment on he knew the reason for mankind's existence, and the value of lessons learned from our reincarnations. He began to give lectures in the town square about his vision of a society based upon optimism and the fact that human beings could be the masters of their own destiny without having to depend on forces outside of themselves. Before long, he had a large group of followers who helped him form the community of Damanhur in 1977."

We were elbowing each other to get a good look at this totem object in hopes that we might also be zapped with enlightenment. However none of us were whisked into a hypnotic trance or seemed to gain sudden wisdom, so we trailed off after our guide—the ladies close on his heels waiting for his next mystical pronouncement while I furiously scribbled notes and attempted to keep up on this whirlwind tour of dusty antiquities.

He suddenly spun around and looked sternly at us. Once he had everyone's attention, he said, "We are about to enter the Hall. No speaking is allowed as it may interrupt others' communion with their memories. It is recommended that you walk very slowly and follow the arrows around the room. Do not go in the opposite direction of the arrows. Stop in front of each statue by yourself, calm your mind, and gaze into each face for several minutes. It may ignite your own past life memories."

Arched wooden doors opened onto to a long hall lined with life-size statues. The arrow-marked path painted on the marble floor circumnavigated the room, passing in front of each statue spaced about three feet apart. As my eyes adjusted to the shadowy light, I could see they were all the same regal personage with very similar facial features and adornments.

He continued, "There are twenty-one statues in this room. They are all of Sekhmet—the lion-headed goddess of Egypt."

His voice faded. Had he really said *"lion-headed goddess"*?

With a sharp intake of breath, I stepped away from the group and leaned against the doorframe.

Just the night before I had had a vivid dream.

Bone-tired but content from teaching a successful dance workshop, I had slipped into a profoundly deep sleep at a student's house in Bologna. In the dream I was walking alone on a forest path high in alpine mountains. The ground was spongy with rust and taupe-colored leaves and pungent pine needles and the air was crisp and sparkling fresh. Strolling peacefully along I had the sudden disturbing sensation of eyes piercing into my back and whirled around. Fifty feet behind me on the trail stood a lion staring at me with glowing eyes. He was stunningly fit with a glossy golden coat, paws as large as pie plates, and a thick tail that swished slowly behind him like a hypnotizing snake. I considered running but knew the lion could overcome me with ease, so I continued staring into his tourmaline eyes. Instantly, the barrier of fear between us dissolved as I looked into the face of my beloved. He sauntered toward me, our gaze unbroken as my heart swelled. He stood up on his powerful back legs, his mane flowing down his back and opened his arms. I could not resist his invitation and we embraced. I was enveloped in the enticing musky, male aroma that emanated from his tawny fur coat. Our attraction was beyond words. We communicated telepathically and both recognized we were soul mates. I was completely viscerally immersed in this knowledge of fathomless love, yet the logical part of me knew that the union of a woman and a lion would not be accepted in society. I would have to build a castle compound on the top of the mountain where we could live together without the interference, cruelty, and judgment of humans.

Waking, I was absolutely certain this was not a mere dream. Tears trickled down my cheeks as I realized how beautiful yet sad this true love was. Yes, we met in the dream world but we were meant to be together in this physical realm, too. His loving eyes followed me internally as I continued on my train journey the next day to Damanhur.

Now, less than twelve hours later, I was standing in front of a human figure with a lion's head. Twenty-one of them! This statue *was* the union of a woman and a lion.

The voice of our tour guide pulled me back into the present moment. Leaning against one of the statues as if they were old friends, he continued his lecture.

"In Egyptian mythology, Sekhmet was originally the warrior goddess as well as the goddess of healing for Upper Egypt. She is depicted as a lioness, the fiercest hunter known to the Egyptians. It was said that her breath created the desert."

"Why is she called Sekhmet?" I asked.

He answered, "Sekhmet's name comes from the ancient Egyptian word *sekhem*, which means 'powerful one.'"

We spent an hour slowly circling the hall, peering into the faces of Sekhmet. It was relaxing, and a wonderful way to interact with the goddess. Though no past life memories were revealed, I did get an inexplicable overwhelming urge to eat pizza.

When we had all gathered outside the hall with the curator, I asked him why the museum had been collecting this particular Egyptian deity—the lion-headed Sekhmet.

He paused, looked at me with his eyebrows pasted high on his forehead, and replied in a semi-snooty tone, "Because we believe she holds the memory of past lives."

He continued, "We wanted her so much that we traded the Rosetta Stone to the British Museum for thirteen statues of Sekhmet."

I whistled and said, "No way. The Rosetta Stone was the key to understanding the hieroglyphs and one of the most important pieces in Egyptian history."

He smiled benignly at me and continued, "We also traded with Egypt a life-size gold statue of Horus, one of the top most important gods in the pantheon of Egyptian deities, for more Sekhmets."

As I jotted details in my Moleskine pocket notebook, my journalistic training took over and I asked in my best reporter voice, "Isn't it unusual for museum directors to be into the esoteric arts and rituals?"

He tugged on his goatee and answered, "Yes,

normally, but not in Turin. Considered one of the top black arts capitals in Europe along with London and Prague, there are more tarot readers, palmists, and alchemists here than in any other region in Italy."

He added, "From a magician's point of view, Turin is a magic reference point in the world. White and black magic are both strong here. It is a chessboard crossed by synchronic lines that also pass through Stonehenge and Giza and are linked to Tibet and Easter Island. Four lines directly cross Damanhur. They converge at the Temple of Humankind."

"A temple of *what*?" I asked.

One of the Brits standing behind me chimed in, "The temple at Damanhur is why our group came to Italy. You are welcome to join us but you will have to participate in the entire three-day program. Walking the Hall of Memory is the first part of our initiation process."

As we left the museum, the curator closed the large doors behind us, then reopened them a crack and said in his deep and splendid voice, "There is an exceptional pizza restaurant around the corner."

Hmm. I had not mentioned craving pizza…

The entire drive back to Damanhur I was haunted by my dream. Aware of being in both worlds at once, I sat in the bus with my new Brit gal pals and simultaneously walked with my lion lover on the forest path.

Back at the retreat, I hurried to the reception desk, anxious to check in, get my suitcase, and have a quick supper at the cafeteria before turning in for the night and hopefully rendezvousing with my lion lover in the dream world. Platypus looked at me over his round spectacles from his perch behind the counter. "How was your museum visit with the sidekicks?"

"I enjoyed their company and they fed me lots of biscuits." I added playfully, "Platypus, it is 'psychics'—not 'sidekicks.'"

He laughed heartily and said, "*Bravissimo!* You will join those sidekicks for the rest of your stay."

With no visitations from my feline lover, I was awakened the next morning by a knock on my door and a cheery British voice. "Dearie, rise and shine—it is time to dance!"

I grabbed my notebook and knocked back an espresso at the cafeteria before joining my adopted tour group. We entered a large, darkened room with a low ceiling. A short, jolly man handed us blindfolds and greeted us. "*Buongiorno*, my name is *Giraffa*. You will dance in the dark for two hours. Don't worry about bumping into anyone. Your other senses will guide you."

I whispered to one of my pudgy, lavender-leotard-wearing dance buddies, "Why does everyone here have such weird names?"

She laughed and then explained, "The citizens of Damanhur choose an animal name in order to affirm their brotherhood with all life forms."

Over the next two days, the lion dream receded as I was swept up in a flurry of occult rituals with my Brits. We danced, we chanted, we walked a stone labyrinth to "align our energies." We witnessed a ceremony where dozens of Damanhurians dressed in long, pastel-colored robes moved in a snail-slow, solemn dance among Ionic columns under the full moon. Despite my Brits' enthusiasm for the experience, it all had the lighthearted air of cosmic children playing at mystic games. I didn't feel particularly altered or evolved—just happy to be in such an aesthetic environment. And it certainly provided fodder for an interesting travel story.

On the third day, we walked the stone labyrinth in silence one last time and then headed up the hillside to the entrance of the Temple of Humankind.

All ten of us were nervous, not knowing what the final initiation ceremony might be—what awaited behind the plain wooden door on the hillside where we gathered, the setting evocative of Bilbo Baggins' beloved Bag End Shire home. This simple door, entrance to the most sacred place in Damanhur, opened without fanfare and our new guide, named *Elefante*, invited us into a small foyer that housed an elevator.

He elaborated on the history of the temple in a hypnotic, sonorous tone. "It was built in secret by hand until 1991, when the local government was tipped off that the residents of Damanhur were building an enormous underground structure. The government officials did not know where it was," Elefante told us, "but they knew it was in this hill, so they threatened to just start bulldozing and dynamiting. We had to give in and let them see it. They then ordered us to destroy the temple because we had built it without their approval. Damanhur alerted the newspapers and the television and the Italian arts community sprang into action. How could Italy, a country that celebrated and worshipped art, halt the construction of the eighth wonder of the world?" he asked.

With a sweeping arm gesture, he invited us to step

into the elevator. We all managed to squeeze in, stuffed to overflowing as it slowly creaked one hundred feet downward. The doors opened into a chamber with elaborate murals and sculpted tree roots symbolizing the first chakra and the beginning of mankind. Elefante explained, "Each level of this temple is an artistic masterpiece and reproduction of the inner rooms of every human being. On one level is the largest Tiffany stained glass domed ceiling in the world."

As we were guided through the labyrinth of opulently carved and painted temple chambers, robed figures glided silently by us without a glance in our direction in the richly decorated, narrow passageways. They all donned Orson Welles copper-wire hats with antennas and other gizmos sticking out. Our guide explained, "These skull caps enhance our ability to receive the river of energies that emanate from the synchronic lines intersecting the temple."

Four hours later, the elevator doors opened to the fading afternoon light on the surface. The usually talkative Brits were nonplussed by the magnitude of art and ritual blended together in the heart of this mountain. We could only shake our heads, speechless—the temple was the most magnificent human structure I'd ever seen. It made the Great Pyramid of Giza seem lifeless, the Golden Gate Bridge ordinary, the art at the Louvre two-dimensional (well, not quite).

That evening, after taking a nap to recharge before leaving Turin, I waved goodbye to my sidekick friends, who chorused, "You *must* come stay with us in England. Perhaps you could change your travel plans and continue on with us?"

Tempting, yes, but it was time to go back home to my reality of family and work. Platypus gave me a lift in his tiny Fiat to the train station in Ivrea near Damanhur. We hugged goodbye as I asked, "Why did you choose the name Platypus?"

He giggled and said, "I like the way they wiggle when they walk."

He looked at me whimsically. "What name would you choose?"

That was easy. "*Leona*...the Lioness."

A few days later, after arriving home in California, I was hiking a forested trail with my friend Jeff, a fellow travel writer who was curious about my trip to Italy. We climbed up the green serpentine spine of Mount Tamalpais along Rocky Ridge Trail. In a redwood glen, we found a small pond and lay on the cool, moist needle carpet. A spring bubbled up near us, filling the air with soft gurgling sounds and a sweet scent.

I recounted the peculiar yet magical artistic nature of Damanhur and its thousand citizens. I also shared the intensity of my soul mate lion dream and encountering the twenty-one lion-headed goddesses at the Egyptian museum in Turin.

We napped, lulled to sleep by the tranquility of tall, gently swaying trees, warm shafts of autumn sunlight, flitting birds high in the canopy, and the song of the softly splashing spring.

Suddenly waking, the sun low and the air bracing, we sat up, yawned, and blinked. Both of us were surprised by how deeply and long we had slept. Jeff stretched his arms above his head and then winced. He shifted to the side and felt around on the ground where he had been lying. "Ouch. What's this?" he said.

He held up something about five inches long that I couldn't quite distinguish in the waning light and brushed off the needles and dirt.

I looked, amused at his pained facial expression, but then froze. I had been expecting to see him holding up a pointy pinecone or a shale shard, not her.

Sekhmet stared back at me from the palm of his hand. An exact plastic replica of the lion-headed goddess seated on a throne.

"Did you bring this with you?" he asked, clearly confused.

Mystified, I said, "No, I don't know where she came from."

As I shook my head, the lines around Jeff shimmered and blurred and my lion dream began to reappear right there in the hills of Marin.

He looked at me, flabbergasted, and said, "Was I really sleeping *on* Sekhmet? I can't believe you told me about a goddess I had never heard about before and then she shows up under my ass!"

## EPILOGUE

When I started writing this story in December of 2012, I was also looking to book an apartment in Paris for a future trip. I found a perfect one in the Marais and made a reservation through an agency. A week later, the owner sent a confirmation email with the name of the apartment: The Sleeping Lion also explaining that it is in a building that housed the lions for King Charles V's menagerie during the 14th century. My lover is still with me. Where will he appear next?

# THE BLUE EYE

Big Island of Hawai'i 2007

Early morning in the Puna District on the rainy side of the Big Island. A sputtering car engine idles in the driveway, competing with the stereophonic coqui frog sing-along and awaking bird choir. My long-time friend Willy Iaukea is grinning from the driver's window and cajoles, "Come on! It's time for an adventure."

He does this often. A truck honk will announce his unexpected arrival, followed by that infectious smile and an invitation to join him on an expedition to some remote part of the island. He knows where the petroglyphs are carved, where the leatherback turtles come to lay their eggs, the terrain that hides lava tube caves with ancient skulls staring back at us along its ledges. He knows the dark, secretive places where the *ali'i*, or royalty, hid during the many tribal wars. I never know where we are headed or when I will return to my home, but I've learned that to not take him up on his offer and hop in his truck for a day of exploration is a day sadly spent. He is my Hawaiian history guide. So what if all that day I have to live on Spam *musubi*—a questionable delicacy composed of a block of rice with a slice of grilled Spam on top and *nori* (seaweed) wrapping to hold it together. It is sold in every gas station and mom & pop grocery store on the island.

So away we go.

Willy loves his hot coffee, his Spam, his cigarettes, and long drives punctuated with "talk story." He is the real deal, a career military guy with deep Hawaiian roots. Willy is from the original stock of navigators and astronomers who arrived in Hawai'i sometime between A.D. 300 and 800 in canoes from Polynesia. Hence he knows everybody on the island, as he is probably related to them in one way or another.

Two hours later, his rusty, reliable truck carries us over the windswept shoulders of Kohala Volcano. We are on a journey to the other side of the Big Island to visit Willy's ancestors. After stopping in Hawi for coffee, we turn onto a rutted dirt road and jounce along for miles on a ribbon of bucking bronco road sloping toward the sea. The track ends abruptly at a barbed-wire fence. Willy pulls his weed whacker out of the truck bed and, in response to my puzzled look, says, "My relatives are buried here. I come every so often to clear the weeds."

I walk to the cliff's edge through cane grass gone wild, like a lion's mane blanketing the hills all the way down to the bluff that drops into the fathomless 'Alenuihaha

Channel that separates Maui from the Big Island. It is a warm, blue day. I sit, hypnotized by the swirling surf below. Finally, Willy joins me and unwinds the story of this isolated, windswept place.

"There was a healing *heiau* [temple] here in the 1700s. Chieftess Keku'iapoiwa, King Kamehameha's mother, was the head *kapuna* [priestess]. Warriors returned, wounded from battle—not just physically, but from what we today call PTSD. They were sent here to mend those inner traumas. The *kapuna* prescribed that they sit right here and stare for days into the ocean where that rock protrudes."

"Why?" I ask. I can't imagine sitting here interminably without hats and sunglasses, but keep myself from saying so. I've learned not to interrupt Willy's storytelling with irreverent witticisms.

"They were not told why," Willy says, "But look at the rock. That place where the rock is located creates a unique phenomenon. Three powerful, surging currents come together. When the tide is right, they clash like titans and spray upward, creating an upside down waterfall or a geyser. The warriors were told to gaze unrelentingly at this, letting the force and imagery pull the shards of painful memory from their minds, releasing them to the sky. It could take weeks."

"Why are your relatives buried here?" I ask.

Willy leads me to the two graves he has cleared just a few feet from the cliff's edge. "My uncles' role was to protect the *ali'i*. One night a chief from Maui sent his men in secret under the cover of night to attack this temple, knowing that King Kamehameha was waiting for them on the battlegrounds at South Point on the other side of the island. King Kamehameha's troops were tricked into leaving their post by this chief, who attacked the *heiau*. Everyone was killed. My uncles died defending Keku'iapoiwa."

We kneel over the burial mounds. There is a crack between the stones in one of the graves. I spontaneously take off my dangly blue earring and drop it in, a gift. We peer into the crevice and stare at the glinting sapphire catching a ray of sun.

"It looks like a whale's eye," I say.

The silence around us is suddenly filled with an enormous whoosh, a cool mist of saltwater spray and an exhale. A wind of breath. We look down at the water, where only twenty feet away two huge humpback whales have breached so high they are looking at us eye-to-eye.

# THE FIRMAMENT OF FOOD

Ashland 2011

As my 89-year-old mother wolfs down a plate of fried oysters and dips slab-cut steak fries in tartar sauce with a gusto she has for no other activity except eating, I ponder, how is this the one thing she remembers at the end of her life? Not tying her shoes or how to turn on the TV, just eating like there is no tomorrow. Was she always such a foodaholic? I have the entire meal to reflect on her one last passion, as she has forgotten how to converse.

Then the phone call comes to mind. It rings in my head like an old-fashioned rotary dial telephone. It was twenty-some years ago when I called to tell her I was leaving my husband. Yes, the same guy Mom and Dad thought was such a catch.

It took days to get the courage up and announce my

heart-wrenching decision. *Gulp.* I dialed my parents' number. Mom answered.

"Mom, I'm leaving Andrew and getting a divorce."

Silence.

"I had a party last night." Her sunshiny voice suddenly came alive over the phone line.

*What?*

She continued, "I made cheese olive balls wrapped in a sharp cheddar pastry crust for hors d'oeuvres."

Stunned, I had no response. And no appetite. I'd already lost ten pounds worrying about the impact of my decision on my financial future and the emotional damage it might do to my 7-year-old son.

Cheese olive balls. Cheese olive balls. It became a weird mantra echoing in my brain. The words looped around a track that has been grooved into my psyche since birth. Do *not* talk about unhappy things.

Silence. Silence. And more silence.

Mom's cheery voice pulled me back once again. "Aha, here is the recipe card. I make two to three times the amount it calls for and then freeze them for when guests come over for drinks. It instructs you to cut the butter into the flour until it is in pea-size chunks and then mash it with your fingers, their warmth softening the butter. Use large, green Spanish pimento-stuffed olives and really sharp Wisconsin cheddar cheese. Roll a small ball of the pastry dough in your palm and then push the olive into the center with your thumb. Press the dough around it, completely wrapping the olive. Bake for fifteen minutes at four hundred degrees."

As she chattered over the phone line, I saw what held

up the firmament that surrounded her fear and barricaded her from her feelings. Food. Beautiful, filling food.

A pause and then she continued, "Absolutely fabulous with dry vermouth gin martinis in chilled stemware. I like to use the glasses that are the size of bathtubs. Absolutely fabulous. Fab.u.lous! Are you there?" She sounded exalted and anxious at the same time.

Silence. Numbness. Disbelief. Was I really listening to a recipe for the smallest, most inconsequential food in the world? An appetizer—not even a main course? Something I would never make. Ab.so.lute.ly useless. My heart was the olive being smothered in buttery crust, a rich orb of yumminess wasted on shallow cocktail conversations.

God, what should I say? Scream at her? Sob into the phone, "I need you now. I'm drowning in sadness and confusion. Who will love me as I destroy the wasteland of my marriage?"

What should I say?

"Have you written all the ingredient amounts down?" Her voice sounded strained.

I finally responded, "No, but the doorbell is ringing and I have to go." And I hung up. And I never called back to ask for that recipe.

For years and years after that phone call made on one of the most miserable days of my life, for years and years after my subsequent divorce, I hated olives. Ab.so.lute.ly hated them. Then, one day, when I was recounting to a friend my feelings of emotional abandonment represented by an olive recipe, I giggled and began to see this vacuous one-way conversation with my mom as humorous.

Much to my surprise, I even started eating those very

same cheese olive balls I resented, savoring their piquant buttery deliciousness. It became a favorite. A must-have that Mom enthusiastically prepared every time I visited her in Oregon. An olive branch of sorts. This was before she started forgetting to turn off the oven; burned vats of soup; scorched the cheese olive ball bottoms. This was before I moved her from her house to the assisted-living wing at the Manor.

Now, Mother's Day 2011, I sit across from her at Larks restaurant in Ashland. She doesn't know where she is or how she got here, but she knows how to eat and it is a marathon of digestive fortitude and commitment. I can't keep up with her. She is a racehorse on the track, rapidly consuming fried oysters, fries, bread, butter, an ice cream sundae, cookies, and champagne.

I realize food is her anchor. Her refuge from a mother who committed suicide, from ten full-term miscarriages, from a criminal son who died young. From a husband who never took care of her and viewed her as his servant.

Suddenly, I understand. And I accept.

She can eat as many Dagoba chocolate sundaes as she wants. I will get over my need to talk talk talk of my inner realm, of my heartbreaks and disappointments.

As the warm chocolate sauce dribbles down her chin and lands like a tear, a faded flower-petal stain on the front of her pink turtleneck, she looks directly at me. Her rheumy eyes shine with happiness even though she can't really see me. I am a shadowy outline, but she is grateful I'm here. Eating eating eating. And that makes it all taste good.

Since her move, I now possess her metal recipe-card

file box. It resides next to towers of cookbooks in my kitchen cupboard. The cheese olive ball index card is stained and tattered around the edges, the words smeared and greasy, barely discernable under layers of buttery fingerprints.

It is time to extract that recipe from its metal strongbox. It is time for me to bake some cheese olive balls and lift my martini glass in a toast to love wrapped in tangy, sharp-cheddar pastry crust.

**Cheese Olive Balls:**
2 cups shredded sharp cheddar cheese
1 ¼ cups flour
½ cup butter, melted
1 jar pimento-stuffed olives

Work cheese and flour together until crumbly. Add butter and mix well with fingers. Mold 1 teaspoon dough around olive; shape into ball. Place 2 inches apart on an ungreased baking sheet. Cover and chill for 1 hour or longer. Heat oven to 400 degrees. Bake 15-20 minutes. Serve hot. Makes 2-3 dozen balls. (Do not use self-rising flour in this recipe.)

# AUTHOR'S NOTE

Phyllis McCreery, my mom, passed away suddenly two weeks after our last Mother's Day together in 2011— just days after I finished writing this story.

# TWO THUMBS UP

New Zealand 2011

The last time I saw my son, I was waving to him through the back window of a decrepit taxi in Chennai, India. Galen called out, "Love you, Mama! Love you!" as the taxi disappeared into the murky night taking me to catch my flight back home to California.

Ten months later, if Galen isn't stuck traversing some gnarly glacier on the South Island, he will be waiting for me at the Christchurch International Airport in New Zealand.

Most people exclaim how difficult it must be for me that my 28-year-old son lives and travels in countries so far from home. On the contrary, I find it exhilarating to meet up with him and explore a new place he has grown to love. "Mother India" embraced him for a year and a half, and then he moved to New Zealand in February of 2011, landing there only three days after a devastating 6.3 earthquake leveled Christchurch.

The plane descends through steel-gray clouds that cap the misty green landscape. I'm glad I brought my ski parka, despite the fact that it's October and supposed to be early summer here.

I gather my bags and make my way through customs with a combination of excitement over the prospect of adventure and a mother's anticipation. In India, my son greeted me wearing a sarong wrapped around his lean body, hair in a topknot, and carrying a long-stem red rose. I wonder how I will find him now.

But he is not at the gate. I wander through the airport to the street, just as a small Toyota drives up with Galen in it, waving and grinning.

A ride, how delightful! I thought we'd be hitchhiking to Golden Bay where he lives, a method of transport I'd agreed to when first making plans, but soon regretted. By the time I realized I'd rather rent a car, rental prices had tripled. I accepted my fate and attempted to meet Galen's enthusiasm that this was the only way to truly meet New Zealanders. "Come on, Mom—you'll love it and it's sooooo easy."

Galen has grown a beard and his long, blond hair flows down his back. He looks like a Viking in his mountain-climbing attire. He envelops me in a huge bear hug and I inhale the scent of campfires and pine trees.

He introduces me to Heidi, the apple-cheeked young woman behind the wheel—the most recent addition to his flock of admirers. He is like honey to bees when it comes to women.

Feeling woozy from the long flight, I beg them for a coffee stop as I want to be clear-headed for this wonderful reunion with my son. Near Heidi's house in Christchurch is a cafe where I buy us large lattés decorated with heart designs floating on their creamy surfaces. Galen has wisely waited for the caffeine to kick in to announce, "We're going to a rave tonight and we want you to come with us."

A rave? I'd been to raves years ago when dancing until sunrise seemed like a fun thing to do. Galen exclaims, "You will love it! Dancing all night long outside with Kiwis."

"What kind of music?" I ask, suspecting that it is the loud, persistent, electronic beat that I have come to associate with an angry washing machine stuck on the rinse cycle—otherwise known as Techno.

"Techno," he confirms.

"Will it be cold?" I ask as I mentally note the snow-capped mountains in the distance.

Galen cheerfully responds, "Yes, and it will probably be raining. It's in a farmer's cow pasture two hours from here. You can sleep in the car if you get tired." Heidi nods vigorously. It's obvious this is her idea to go to the rave with Galen in tow, though I wonder if she knew his mom would be tagging along.

A few hours later, Galen and three other friends are trying on various costumes at Heidi's house. She is a preschool teacher by day and, it appears, a rainbow person in the off hours. They suit up in layers of wild print shirts, sparkly skirts, polka dot leggings, and earthy, long, felt vest coats topped with rainbow-striped caps. Heidi sews a lot of the apparel swirling around me, I discover, and I observe the fashion show with great amusement from a beanbag chair with a calico cat purring loudly on my lap.

They morph into over-sized hobbits in hippie wear and I flash back to the Haight-Ashbury days of my youth when they ask, in unison, "What do you want to wear?"

My true desire is a flannel nightgown to cuddle into after a hot bath, followed by a journey into a feather bed, but that doesn't seem to be in my future for this first day in New Zealand. I don't voice this thought but politely decline the offer to dress up like a character from *The Cat in the Hat*, and remain in my unfashionable black ski parka to ward off the bone-chilling cold.

We all crowd into Heidi's car, somehow managing to pack in costumes, food, camping gear, and my roller bag. Windy streets take us past fallen cathedrals and leaning office towers and, even in my foggy, jetlagged condition, I register how terribly devastated the city is from the recent earthquake.

It is a relief to reach the countryside where sheep wander in verdant pastures and meandering rows of spring-green willows fringe creek beds. As we come closer to our destination, I spot a handwritten sign low on the side of the road with the magic letters B&B.

"U-turn! Make a U-turn," I shout from the back seat. Without questioning my impulsive demand, Heidi executes a magnificent turn, accelerating with flair down the muddy road.

At the end of the road sits a modern farmhouse. I ring the bell and a woman greets me as if I am expected, taking control of my roller bag while I follow her to a suite with large picture windows looking out over the vineyards. It is warm and cozy inside, and Galen sweetly agrees not to forget where they have parked me, promising to pick me up the next morning.

I savor a luxuriously long, hot shower, dress, and join the proprietors, Betty and Fred, for a fruity glass of sauvignon blanc beside the fire as we debate the upcoming Rugby World Cup final to be held in Auckland the next evening.

As I lie down on the king-size bed, a heating pad melts my fatigued muscles. I have not slept for 48 hours. A sense of peace pervades and a big grin spreads across my face. Galen is off doing what he wants to do and I am exactly where I want to be. That, my friends, is the difference between being in your twenties versus your late fifties. And to two free spirits, the success of traveling together is that we both get to do what we want.

At nine a.m. sharp, as I am finishing my orange-yolked eggs and thick, crispy bacon, Galen and his circus troupe arrive. The kids' faces are painted and their outfits are askew, but they don't look fatigued. I hug Betty and Fred goodbye and off we go.

That wasn't bad. For $100 I got a wing in their house, wine, dinner, great conversation, breakfast—and a cure for jet lag.

"How was the rave?" I ask.

"We stayed up all night dancing, but I'm glad you didn't come. You wouldn't have liked all the drunks, or the music."

Heidi and friends drop us off on the side of the road just a few miles from the B&B. They drive back to

Christchurch and we hitchhike to Golden Bay, a progressive agricultural community perched on the north end of the South Island. My son has been living there for six months WWOOFing (World Wide Opportunities on Organic Farms) and selling homemade feijoa preserves and chai at the farmers' market.

His insistence that we hitchhike was born from a desire to show me his new home through the locals we'd meet. I'd reluctantly agreed because it had been successful in getting him all over New Zealand and added to his vast collection of friends around the globe.

It is definitely a stretch for me to be standing here beside the tarmac with my roller bag, smiling at potential rides. Last hitchhiking experience? Guatemala, 17 years ago. The Mayan Indians threw rocks at me from the local bus window.

Galen insists I remove my Angelina Jolie sunglasses and stick my thumb out, even when he disappears into the bushes to pee. Several dozen cars pass. So far, hitching does not seem as easy as he claims. Finally a van stops, full of blokes. Much to my relief (as I do not savor the idea of riding with seven guys), just as we run up to the van, they screech off, laughing and pointing at us. Ha ha ha.

One hour later—thank goodness, because Galen and I are beginning to have disagreements about this hitching business—a sputtering, tiny two-door car pulls up. The smiling middle-aged woman driving wears a lavender dress and strings of amethyst beads, and she is very excited about meeting foreigners. We stuff ourselves into her car and drive north. She is fascinated that I'm Galen's mom and have agreed to hitchhike. We trade travel stories—she tells us that she has "only" been to Cambodia to do volunteer medical work, which, for some reason, she does not consider a travel experience. We are impressed with her heartfelt descriptions of the pain she experienced in Cambodia when helping people traumatized by Pol Pot's regime. Galen traveled in Cambodia two years earlier and we actually spill tears as the two of them discuss their interactions with people who were so open yet scarred by that period of history.

She drops us at the turnoff for Lewis Pass, which is still 300 kilometers from our destination. Before long, a trucker gives us a lift. We sit in the front cab, looking across the country through a gigantic picture windshield that provides us a full panoramic view of the mountains. The trucker is a roadie on his way to Nelson to pick up sound equipment after the Rugby World Cup festivities tonight. He loves his job and tells us stories about carting sound equipment for U2's recent tour in New Zealand. He hung out with Bono backstage—a roadie's raison d'être.

Halfway to Nelson, which is at the top of the South Island and at least four hours further, the roadie leaves us in the whitewater rafting town of Murchison. The Backpacker Hotel has a cheery room for us with stellar valley views, and the River Café dishes up lamb shank pie and a pint; then it's off to the pub for the rugby finale. Galen is hoping for a crowd of rowdy, ruddy-cheeked farm boys in gumboots yelling in drunken enthusiasm but it is disappointingly subdued and quiet for a workingman's pub. The All Blacks win, but the triumph is far tougher than expected, with the All Blacks barely squeezing by France, 8-7. Even after several polite blokes at the bar explain rugby to me, I still don't understand the game and all that butt-hugging scrimmaging that wins it.

We're back on the road the next morning, and the young couple who picks us up lead kayak tours along the Abel Tasman coastline. We play a game that requires we shout, "Tractor!" whenever we spot one. Our conversation about tramping in Abel Tasman National Park, and our driver's recent arrest for defending a woman who got beaten up by her boyfriend (the other guy's face "will never look the same"), is frequently punctuated by "Tractor!" Points accumulate fast, as New Zealand is one big farm spread.

"Would you like to go for a swim?" the driver asks.

To me this seems odd, as it is freezing outside, but we agree to the adventure and they take us on a detour to the Resurgence. I wonder if we are going to a religious revival and baptism, but it is a magical forest where a crystal-clear river spills out of a limestone cave and pours down the valley. Our new friends tell us it is a sacred and ancient place where the Maori came to give birth. The water is icy but we get naked, dive in, and swim to the rocks like speedboats to emerge shivering but exhilarated.

Back on the road, we stop to buy fresh asparagus from a produce stand and gift our drivers a bunch, too. After goodbye hugs they leave us at the turnoff for the road that leads over the hill to Golden Bay, which we'll reach, hopefully, in the next day or two.

When a giant green school bus stops, it takes us a moment to realize that the elderly couple who motion us to hop in are the drivers. We settle into sheepskin-covered banquettes and the lady tells us proudly that this is their new home. They just sold their farm to live in this bus as they explore the country. They say they have not traveled much, and then the woman casually adds, "We are also missionaries and lived with the Huli Wigmen clan in the Southern Highlands of Papua New Guinea for ten years. We raised our four children in that remote region, a two-day hike from anywhere."

Our jaws hang open at this account of these intrepid, friendly farmer folk. As they drop us off near our final destination, the wife winks at me and says, "I always really wanted to be a hippie."

Five rides, two days, and a multitude of conversations later, we arrive in Takaka in Golden Bay at the Grove Orchard where Galen lives. We set up camp beside the creek, as my son has always preferred living outdoors no matter what the temperature. I can't complain since I'm the one who taught him how to travel the world. Starting when he was eight months old, we camped with Berbers in Morocco, hitchhiked in Bali, rode horseback through the snowy passes in the Sierra Nevada— generally wandering the world like gypsies. But I'm several decades older now, and long for that B&B with 1,000-thread-count sheets and a glass of wine next to a cozy fireplace.

Galen reads my mind. He builds a wood fire beneath the porcelain bathtub under the stars and fills it with buckets of cold creek water. He pours me a fine glass of white wine, and when the tub starts to steam I sink in, marveling at the constellations above, unrecognizable to me in this different hemisphere, traveling like a gypsy again.

# EPILOGUE

Albania 2013

*On distant shores lies treasure, food, and friends.*
— Gulliver's Travels

What is the reward for finishing these stories that give muscle, bone, and sinew to *Wild Life*? A grand adventure to somewhere I'd never been. A place mysterious—perhaps dangerous... .

Dogs terrify me.
A pack of barking dogs unseen but heard approach us

179

as we walk on the gravel road back to the Hotel Livia. It is an inky black night in the countryside of Butrint, Albania. The full moon late to rise.

Dogs with bared fangs in foreign countries are the most terrifying. Albania is not known for its modern medical facilities. The Bradt guidebook advises travelers to go to the military hospital in the capital of Tirana and warns that rabies are endemic.

Meanwhile, I ready the only weapon in reach—a jangling money belt filled with Albanian lek—to clout the beasts over the muzzle. In despair, I imagine a big-jawed mutt capturing a nylon strap in its teeth, playing tug-of-war, my hands inches from its salivating mandibles.

Jordan, my sweet love and knight in shining armor, pulls out his iPhone and, *voila!*, activates the flashlight app. The dogs slink into the scrub oak forest.

My heartbeat slows as a bronze-faced moon rises over the rim of Corfu, just two kilometers across the channel, lighting our way.

In blogs and guidebooks, we were warned about the perils of travel in Albania: gigantic ankle-twisting potholes, finger-busting gangsters, nothing to eat but 27 types of meatballs, no hot water, insane drivers, no English spoken.

All untrue.

Albania turns everything on its ear that is written about it. We encounter no thugs, no meatballs, and find plenty of hot water, safe drivers, and English spoken. Sure, there are a few potholes. And poisonous snakes, of which we've seen four, including the deadly Ursini's Viper.

We rely on the travel mercies of the Albanian people

as we explore their country via foot and public transport. The care and attention they offer us is remarkable, even though we speak only a few words of Albanian. "Po" means "yes," and a hand on the heart is a blessing mixed with "thank you."

That is all we need besides our money belt and a smartphone. And a large dose of trust and curiosity about all things human and earthy; dreamlike and inexplicable.

# ABOUT THE AUTHOR

Lisa Alpine is the award-winning author of *Exotic Life: Travel Tales of an Adventurous Woman* (winner of a BAIPA Book Awards Best Women's Adventure Memoir). She co-authored *Wild Writing Women: Stories of World Travel* and the first edition of the *Self-Publishing Boot Camp Workbook*.

Writing, dancing, gardening, yoga, hiking, family, and travel are the passions of her life. She divides her time between Mill Valley, California and the Big Island of Hawai'i.

Find out about her writing workshops and book events at www.lisaalpine.com.

## AUTHOR'S NOTE

In the photo I'm soaking in a remote sulfuric hot spring near Përmet, Albania. A stone bridge built by Ali Pasha during the Ottoman Empire arcs in the distance.

# NOTE TO THE ASPIRING WRITER

I try to look normal, but I am a writer, and we are a convoluted breed. I liken my writing process to mud wrestling. I sweat, get ugly, and slump too long at the keyboard. I routinely ignore my family and friends. With my unkempt hair and fuzzy bathrobe the only props missing are an ashy cigarette dangling from the corner of my mouth and a highball glass with bourbon sloshing onto my manuscript.

> *Writing is like ballet. A ballerina looks like she's levitating, but look at her feet and they're bleeding.*
> — Barbara Kingsolver

When the words that spill out are finally wrestled into the storyline, I am ecstatic. Maybe those words are an absolutely accurate description of a blazing sunset. Maybe they're telling of a moment of truth when I hear the river's scream and yawl, and I point my kayak toward the hypnotic invitation of peaked rapids.

Mood-enhancing endorphins are released when a writer delves deep into an experience and returns with her verbal quarry—the perfectly constructed story where every word has auditioned for the page.

At least, it feels that way to me.

And then I take a shower.

*Don't bend; don't water it down; don't try to make it logical; don't edit your own soul according to the fashion. Rather, follow your most intense obsessions mercilessly.*
— Franz Kafka

This is the advice Cheryl Strayed, the author of *Wild*, gave at a writing workshop I attended. Yes, I still have "beginner's mind" and take writing workshops—not just teach them.

There is no finish line stating "greatness" for the writer. And I have faced the valleys of sloth and criticism. Rejection? I know rejection and its smirky face.

Several decades ago I took a workshop with a well-known author who teaches the craft of writing. She invited students to bring in a story to read. I read my story and afterward, there was a moment of silence.

"That sucks!" the teacher finally pronounced.

Permission thus granted, the other students dove on me like jackals. "I've been to Bali and it's not like that at all!" "Why is it so happy and everything is so pretty?"

I walked out in shock.

That evening my self-doubt transformed into anger. My Bali story wasn't that bad! Certainly, it was better than many of the other pieces read and none of the other students got their heads chewed off.

"Oh, yeah?" I thought, and I printed it out and sent it to the *San Francisco Examiner & Chronicle* travel section.

A few days later Don George, the editor, called me. He loved it and its happy, sensual tone. It appeared that same month on the front page of the Sunday travel section.

Don inadvertently launched my travel writing career just as I was about to abort the mission. I also give credit to that writing instructor, and have thought to personally thank her when next I see her waiting in line at the Fairfax post office. I would tap her shoulder and say, "Thank you for kick-starting my career (in the ass). I'd probably still be working on that story today if my hackles hadn't risen!"

And we would laugh. At least I would.

*I make up my own mind about [the work] — how good or bad or indifferent it is. After that, critics can write what they please. I have already settled it for myself so flattery and criticism go down the same drain and I am quite free.*
— Georgia O'Keeffe

Advice to you, dear reader: view rejection and frustration as the matador's cape. The matador's sword will pierce you. After, think about it. Do you really want to be a writer? If so, stand up and dust yourself off. Stamp and paw and snort and charge again until you knock that matador off his feet with your stunning words.

## Winner of the BAIPA Book Award for Best Women's Adventure Memoir

"*Exotic Life* is a sprawling anthology of 19 travel tales. Alpine is an inspiration to women travelers everywhere. She fearlessly wanders through one obscure destination after the other, leaving her complete trust in the experience. She answers that timeless question – Can solo women travelers really go there? – by doing just that and carrying away some wildly unique stories."   —Rolf Potts' Vagabonding

"Lisa's travels are more than exotic. They are wonderful reading. I have to say this book stayed with me for a long time, and I loved the last three lines about Guadeloupe." —20th Annual Writer's Digest Annual Self-Published Book Awards review

*Exotic Life: Travel Tales of an Adventurous Woman*
Product details: $12.95 print book. $6.99 ebook. 196 pages
Published by Dancing Words Press 2010 & 2014
ISBN-13: 9780984229338

Available in paperback and ebook wherever books are sold.

60888355R00129

Made in the USA
San Bernardino, CA
13 December 2017